AS IF THE HEART MATTERED

A WESLEYAN SPIRITUALITY

GREGORY S. CLAPPER

UPPER ROOM BOOKS

Cover Art Direction: Michele Wetherbee
Cover Illustration: Susan Gross
Cover Design: Laura Beers
Interior Photograph: Rus Baxley
Interior Design: Nancy Cole
First Printing: November 1997 (5)

The Upper Room Web Site: http://www.upperroom.org

The Library of Congress Cataloging-in-Publication Data

Clapper, Gregory Scott.
    As if the heart mattered / Gregory S. Clapper.
        p. cm.
    Includes bibliographical references.
    ISBN 0-8358-0820-3
    1. Spirituality—Methodist Church—History—18th century. 2.
Spirituality—Great Britain—History—18th century. 3. Spiritual life—
Christianity. 4. Wesley, John, 1703-1791—Contributions in spirituality. 5.
Wesley, Charles, 1707-1788—Contributions in spirituality. 6. Methodist
Church—Great Britain—Doctrines—History—18th Century. 7. Great
Britain—Church history—18th century. I. Title.
BX8276.C63 1997
248.08827—dc21   97-11415
                                                                   CIP

Printed in the United States of America

For Laura and Jenna
Gifts from God

Contents

Why Should Anyone Care about a "Wesleyan" Spirituality?

 This book is designed to give the reader a solid grounding in the spirituality, or "heart religion," of John Wesley. We will not look *at* Wesley as a person so much as we will look *with* him. This means that I will not be rehearsing Wesley's own spiritual development, but instead will share his vision of how Christian faith is embodied in that central core of what we think, what we will, and what we feel—in short, the deepest center of who we are: the human heart.

In What Way Is This a "Wesleyan" Spirituality?

This is a "Wesleyan" spirituality for two reasons. The first is that it is scripturally based. I will use the Bible as my main reference. This seems the most appropriate method for a study in the tradition of a man who thought of himself as *homo unius libri*—a man of one book (i.e., the Bible). I will focus on scriptural passages (including many that Wesley himself emphasized) to describe the basic building blocks of the Christian life. References to John Wesley's own works—and to the hymns of his brother Charles Wesley—will be given for the interest of those who want to pursue certain issues in more depth, but scripture will be my touchstone.

The second reason this is a "Wesleyan" spirituality is that I will be guided in my interpretation of scripture by the Wesleyan interpretive tradition, a tradition that reflects Wesley's wide and deep reading as an Oxford fellow and lecturer. This "man of one book" read hundreds of other books in order to help him interpret the most important book. Based on his extensive reading, Wesley's theology emphasized two fundamental elements of the Christian tradition: God's initiating grace and humanity's freedom to respond to this grace. I will show these elements in action in the biblical passages I interpret rather than make them the subject of a self-conscious theoretical elaboration. This book, therefore, will not be an exercise in polemics, eagerly showing how the Wesleyan tradition might differ from some others. Instead I will simply portray in a positive way this broad and strong branch of the Christian tradition.

The Wesleyan interpretive tradition will be most obvious through the use of an image that Wesley used to describe the essentials of both Christian doctrine and the Christian life. This image is that religion is like a house. The three main parts of Wesley's "house of religion" are repentance, faith, and holiness. Each of these foundational themes will be the focus of one chapter, and unpacking the richness of this "house" image will be the heart of the book.

Before we begin exploring this image, I wish to make a few remarks about the biblical basis of this work and about taking Wesley's theology as our guide to biblical interpretation.

Why Should a Spirituality Be Biblically Based?

John Wesley thought that the Bible contained all the information that was necessary for a person to be rightly related to God. In writing a "spirituality" (or a guide to the Christian life) in the tradition of John Wesley, I have depended, as he did, on the truths found in the scriptures. In this emphasis on the importance of scripture, of course, Wesley was hardly unique in the Christian tradition. In fact, this emphasis on scripture puts him in the mainstream of orthodox understandings of Christianity.

Other spiritual seekers, however, such as the Deists in Wesley's time—and many people in our own day—do not look to the Bible in their spiritual quest. Let us, then, briefly explore this question of why we should take the time and effort to construct a biblically based spirituality. This I do especially for the purpose of inviting those unaccustomed to the Bible to give it a serious try.

First of all, we need not preface the discussion of the Bible with intimidating theories about its "infallibility" or "inerrancy." Discussions around those words usually yield little light and much heat, and they are usually incomprehensible for anyone outside of the Christian community (and for many inside!). I want to start with a humbler but very suggestive approach.

H. A. Nielsen in his helpful little book *The Bible: As If for the First Time*[1] used a phrase that gets to the root of why people should take the Bible seriously in their spiritual quests. He said that "rumors of nourishment" surround the Bible, and that these rumors should invite the hungry seeker to try it. For thousands of years, people have been spiritually nourished by the collection of stories, character studies, words of wisdom, prophecies, songs, poems, and moral teachings that the Christian community calls the Bible. By prayerfully searching this diverse collection of literature, the Christian community finds the nature of God and the nature of humanity revealed. We need to be drawn by nothing more fancy or involved than these "rumors of nourishment" to start on our journey of a biblically based spirituality.

Those who already identify themselves as being in the Christian tradition may not need these teasing "rumors of nourishment" in order to explore the Bible, but sometimes Christians also have ideas about the Bible that prevent them from getting the most out of the scriptures. Sometimes

Christians are so immersed in studying the Bible, are so used to hearing its familiar cadences and phrases, that they lose sight of the real purpose of the book.

If one observed the various Bible studies, Sunday school classes, and sermons to which people are exposed, one might think that the main point of being a Christian is to know, perhaps even memorize, as much of the Bible as possible. This is a fundamental mistake. To understand more clearly the nature and purpose of the Bible, let us look at a key passage in the Bible itself and also at a helpful quote by one of Christianity's most influential theologians.

The passage in 2 Timothy 3:16-17 reads as follows: "All scripture is inspired by God and is useful for teaching, for reproof, for correction, and for training in righteousness, so that everyone who belongs to God may be proficient, equipped for every good work."

Here we clearly see that scripture is not an end in itself. Instead, it is to be used for "teaching" (for instance, about who God is and who humanity is); for "reproof" and "correction" (that is, for helping people get back "on track" when they have fallen away from the Christian life); and for training in "righteousness"—in short, for the task of spiritual formation. We should study the Bible not just to pile up more quotations in our head, but we should become more biblically informed so that our whole lives will become congruent with the vision of God and humanity revealed in scripture. When our lives are so formed, we will be "equipped for every good work," ready to be the people that God calls us to be so that we can do what God calls us to do.

Saint Augustine, Bishop of Hippo (354–430) in his powerful little book *On Christian Doctrine* wrote that the purpose of the Holy Scripture is to develop the virtues of faith, hope, and love. He even said that if the believer has an unshakable hold on faith, hope, and love, he or she no longer needs the Bible, except for the instruction of others.[2] While this might sound radical and scary to some, I think it underlines the fundamental point of the passage from Second Timothy, which is that the Bible does not exist for its own sake; rather, it exists for spiritual formation. That is the use to which I will put the Bible in this book.

But if the Bible is to be used to shape human lives, the question immediately arises: How do we arrange and digest this welter of material in the Bible in order to shape a human life? According to what plan is the material to be organized? Where do we find an interpretive foundation on which to build our lives?

The most direct answer is "from the Bible itself." But we need the Holy Spirit if we are to discern this pattern of life from amongst all of the stories, laws, prophecies, parables, letters, and the like. Since the Holy Spirit did not come into the world for the first time in our generation, we can gain guidance in our quest for an orienting pattern by examining how the Bible has been used throughout the Christian tradition to form human lives. Anyone who has studied the Christian tradition, however, will know that it is like a broad and deep river with many branches and not a few stagnant pools. Why is one branch of the river to be preferred over another?

Wesley As a Spiritual Guide

In our present age, there are very good reasons for reaching out to believers of all denominations and for breaking down barriers between one Christian and another. People are increasingly trying to find beliefs and missions in common. Why, then, should anyone look into what one particular thinker in the Christian tradition had to say? Some would shy away from such an enterprise especially because the thinker is famous for having started a movement that led to the development of a new set of denominations, namely, those in the broad "Methodist" tradition! They would fear that this focus on such a person represents a parochial and provincial retreat to narrow denominational competition, circling the wagons against the "outsiders." But this is not what I have in mind.

There are good reasons for all Christians to explore the vision of the Christian life that John Wesley offered. The first reason is that one cannot gain access to the "general" Christian tradition except through one particular branch of the tradition. Trying to be a Christian without starting in some specific tradition is like saying you want to play baseball "in general" but do not want to join a team. It cannot be done!

People who claim to be basing their lives on the Bible alone, with no "interference" from "human traditions," are themselves usually indebted to some preacher or Bible teacher for the views that they have, though they may not be consciously aware of it. We cannot avoid living out of a particular tradition. The best we can do is to be aware of the tradition out of which we are in fact living. With such self-awareness comes the capability to compare, choose, and ask critical questions about our various traditions.

Now that we realize that we have to start somewhere in particular, let us answer the question: Why start with Wesley's theology? Understanding who he was provides one answer to that question.

John Wesley not only spent his whole life thinking about Christianity, he also tried to embody the truth of Christianity and to give institutional shape to this vision. A child of the parsonage, an Oxford teacher, a missionary, a field preacher, a counselor, and a spiritual friend to hundreds—all of these experiences strengthened and focused his conception of what it means to be a Christian, and they fitted him to the task of spiritual mentor and guide.

Another reason to look to Wesley for guidance is apparent when we consider the fruit of this Wesleyan tradition. Given Christianity's two-thousand-year history, any interpretive method that one could bring to the Bible more than likely has been tried before. Some methods have been more helpful than others. Wesley's view clearly is one of the tried and true approaches. Millions of people, as evidenced by the membership of those churches in the tradition of John Wesley, have found that Wesley's understanding of Christianity leads to a life-changing encounter with Jesus. The movement he started has borne rich fruit.

The problem with those in the Methodist (or Methodist-related) traditions that descended from his reform movement is that many who are (in name) a part of the tradition are not aware of the richness that it holds. Wesley's theology is often studied only scantly. Even then, it often is not consciously translated from the classroom or the pulpit into the lives of the individual students or congregants. In other words, though Wesley's theology has indirectly influenced millions, most do not know how and in what way this influence has occurred. Studying Wesley's approach will allow many to name and claim the theological heritage that they have been living unknowingly.

Another reason to take Wesley's vision of the Christian life as our interpretive framework is that his stance is always humbly open to the correction of others. On this point, we need to remember that John Wesley held that "The gospel of Christ knows of no religion, but social; no holiness but social holiness."[3] There is no such thing as a solitary Christian for Wesley. We need each other to discern God's truth, and we cannot rely solely on introspective self-exploration that can easily turn narcissistic. Wesley's heart religion is, by its very nature, open to the correction of the scriptures, the Christian tradition, and the present Christian community.

Wesley saw that to be committed to the truth as we know it while also being humbly open to the views of others is one of the ways that we are called to live out the biblical injunction to "speak the truth in love" (Eph. 4:15). As sinful and broken human beings, we most often would like to do either one or the other: either speak the truth or be loving. But God, through scripture, calls us to do both. In loving others, we are humbly open to hear and consider what they say. At the same time, to maintain our own integrity, we must speak the truth as we perceive it and not unthinkingly capitulate to whatever anyone else says.

To take a "Wesleyan" approach to the spiritual life, then, is to commit oneself to the open and communal crucible of truth known as the body of Christ, where God's truth for us is discerned and our spiritual lives are formed. The communal nature of the body of Christ means that diving into the broad stream of the Christian tradition in the "Wesleyan" branch necessarily opens us up to the other influences, currents, and eddies of the Christian tradition. Taking Wesley's vision of the Christian life leaves us neither so closed off as to be "parochial" nor so "open-minded" as to be "empty-minded." In the end, my interest—like Wesley's interest before me—is not to produce "Wesleyans" as much as it is to produce "Christians." In that spirit I invite the reader to give Wesley's vision of Christianity an open-minded reading.

Overview of This Book

In the first chapter I will explain some of the formal features of Wesley's understanding of a Christian heart religion in order to show how it can fulfill what most hope for in a heart religion while avoiding those things that most people fear. In the next three chapters I will focus on what Wesley termed the three most basic features of a Christian heart religion: repentance, faith, and love. In the last chapter I will share some of Wesley's practical advice concerning how such a heart religion is formed and strengthened and how it is to be expressed and lived out in the world.

To foster a truly Wesleyan understanding of the Christian life, I have included at the end of each chapter references to some of John Wesley's sermons and a brief look at one of Charles Wesley's hymns that is pertinent to the topic covered in the chapter. The hymn numbers refer to the *United Methodist Hymnal* (UMH). I also have included several questions either for discussion (if the book is to be used in a group study) or simply for individual contemplation and reflection. These questions are designed to help the reader engage the realities of one's own heart, in light of John Wesley's understanding of a heart religion, so that one can begin to embody this vision of God's wondrous grace.

Acknowledgments

I want to acknowledge the people who helped this book come about. In addition to the staff at Upper Room Books, I want to thank the leaders, faculty, and my fellow participants in the Two-Year Academy for Spiritual Formation (academy number five), sponsored by The Upper Room. I have been asked to speak on Wesleyan and Protestant Spirituality at subsequent Five-Day and Two-Year Academies across the country, and the material in this book owes much to the give-and-take of these academies.

I also wish to thank the people of Trinity United Methodist Church in Waverly, Iowa, First United Methodist Church of Montgomery, Alabama, and Auburn United Methodist Church, Auburn, Alabama, for asking me to present programs on the topic of Wesleyan Spirituality. A series I taped for Frazer Television (a ministry of Frazer United Methodist Church,

Montgomery, Alabama) on this topic also contributed to the focusing and refining of this work as did a series of talks I gave at Whitfield United Methodist Church, Montgomery, Alabama.

Mrs. Marie Benson deserves a special word of thanks for her endowment of the Chapman Benson Chair of Christian Faith and Philosophy at Huntingdon College which I have the privilege of holding.

Finally, I want to thank my wife, Jody, for her love and support. My dedication of this book to our two daughters reflects not only the joy I experience by having them in my life but also the gratitude I feel for the mother who has helped to shape their hearts.

Notes

[1] *The Bible: As If for the First Time*, H. A. Nielsen (*Spirituality and the Christian Life Series:* vol. I; Philadelphia: Westminster Press, 1984). On approaching the Bible for spiritual formation, see also Thomas Merton's *Opening the Bible* (Collegeville, MN: The Liturgical Press, 1970) and M. Robert Mulholland, Jr.'s *Shaped By the Word: The Power of Scripture in Spiritual Formation* (Nashville, TN: The Upper Room, 1985).

[2] *On Christian Doctrine, Augustin of Hippo, Nicene and Post-Nicene Fathers of the Christian Church*, First Series, vol. II, chapter 39 (Grand Rapids, MI: Wm. B. Eerdmans Publishing Co., 1956).

[3] Preface to 1739 *Hymns and Sacred Poems*, John and Charles Wesley, from *The Works of John Wesley* (Jackson edition), vol. 14, 321.

Chapter One

Fears and Hopes about a Religion of the Heart

The Human "Heart" and "Heart Religion"

 When the authors of scripture—and John Wesley—used the term *heart*, they typically were not referring to the muscle that pumps blood throughout the body. They instead used the term to refer to the center of a human being, that core of who we are. The heart is the source of our strongest desires and the guide for our deepest choices, the home of our most intense yearnings and of our greatest hopes, fears, loves, and dreams. The heart carries our identity, that sense of who we are that is composed of both our history (how we have been formed in the furnace of life up to this point) and our vision of what we want to become (how we hope to be formed in the future). The heart is a metaphor for who we really are, that vision of self we see when, in our frankest moments of honesty and insight, we name what we are really after in life, what brings our greatest fulfillment.

This use of metaphor is hardly unusual in religious language for we can find numerous metaphors scattered throughout the discourses of Jesus as the Bible records them. One bundle of metaphors can be found in the Gospel of John where Jesus describes himself as "the bread of life" (John 6:35), "the good shepherd" (John 10:14), and "the true vine" (John 15:1). These passages show that there is nothing intellectually suspect or sloppy about using a metaphor. Indeed, Jesus' use of these figures of speech shows that sometimes the only way to speak about important realities is through metaphor. However, we also must acknowledge that many people have some bad associations with the particular metaphor on which we will be focusing in this book, namely, "heart." Even more negative are some people's associations with the phrase *heart religion*.

When I have spoken around the country on the topic of Wesleyan heart religion, one of the first things I do is ask people to make two lists of free associations with the phrase *heart religion*. First, I ask them to list all of the positive connotations they associate with the phrase. In answer to this, I often receive responses such as the following: inner fulfillment; a religion that brings together our emotions and our beliefs without denying one or the other; something that reaches beyond the dead recitation of the creeds or a moralistic understanding of religion; a satisfying of our deepest desires; something that brings about a lasting love and joy and peace.

After several minutes of such sharing, there is a noticeable warming of the atmosphere and most people seem eager to pursue the task at hand. But then when I ask people to name the negative connotations of "heart religion" the energy level elevates drastically! There is usually no hesitancy in naming such things as these: irrationality; self-deception; individualism; authoritarian, shame-based manipulation; a self-absorbed religion of feeling; a vision of Christianity that ignores our social life and our connections with both other believers and those outside of the church. Years of pain, fear, and anger start rolling out of people when I ask them to name the possible problems of a heart religion. To one observing these reactions, it can be seen as a therapeutic moment, but such pain-filled statements are also a crushing indictment of much of our church life.

It is in response to both these hopes for, as well as the many well-founded fears about, "heart religion" that I want to make clear what John Wesley meant by this phrase. His was a powerful yet balanced vision, a view that drew on both an Oxford fellow's knowledge of the Christian tradition as well as a humble sinner's own spiritual experience. Wesley's understanding of the spiritual life was further refined and strengthened by his many years of leading a reform and renewal movement in which he had to deal with just about every possible extreme, mistake, and problem of Christian living.

John Wesley's Vision of Heart Religion—Orthokardia[1]

John Wesley affirmed the orthodoxy of the classical creeds of the church, those capsule summaries of Christian doctrine which describe God, humanity, and salvation in brief but powerful words. However, Wesley knew that the "Christianity" that can be put down on paper does not tell the whole story. He also affirmed, espoused, and practiced what has come to be called in the twentieth century *orthopraxis*, or right action. This is to say that he recognized that certain actions are necessary if one is to consider oneself a Christian. These actions he termed the "works of piety" (e.g., taking the sacraments, attending worship, praying, searching the scriptures) and the "works of mercy" (or "works of charity," e.g., visiting those imprisoned, feeding the hungry, clothing the naked, entertaining or assisting the stranger, comforting the afflicted).[2] I will say more about these two different kinds of "works" in a later chapter. What makes Wesley's vision of Christianity different from many others, though, is something that cannot be captured by either *orthopraxis* or *orthodoxy* (right belief). This element is what I have elsewhere termed *orthokardia* ("right heart").[3] (For a fuller explanation of these terms, see the glossary.)

Though Wesley himself never used the term orthokardia, he never stopped proclaiming the "religion of the heart." A full listing of Wesley's references to "heart religion" would run to many pages, but let me give just two here to make the point.

Biblical scholars seem to agree that the key concept in the teaching of Jesus recorded in the Gospels is the "kingdom of God." Jesus proclaimed throughout his life that God's kingdom is "at hand" and we are called to live in it. But what is this "kingdom of God"? Wesley explains:

> This is that kingdom of heaven or of God which is "within us," even "righteousness, and peace, and joy in the Holy Ghost." And what is righteousness but the life of God in the soul, the mind which was in Christ Jesus, the image of God stamped upon the heart, now renewed after the likeness of him that created it? What is it but the love of God because he first loved us, and the love of all mankind for his sake?
>
> And what is this peace, the peace of God, but that calm serenity of soul, that sweet repose in the blood of Jesus, . . .
>
> This inward kingdom implies also "joy in the Holy Ghost," who seals upon our hearts "the redemption which is in Jesus." The righteousness of Christ, imputed to us for "the remission of the sins that are past."[4]

This striking sermon is included in the "Standard Sermons," those sermons that Wesley used to give basic theological guidance to the Methodist Societies. In this sermon, Wesley defines life in the kingdom of God in terms of the life of the heart, which is the seat of love, peace, and joy. That this was a consistent emphasis of his can be seen in many places. Suffice it to point out here that at the end of his thirteen-part series of sermons on the Sermon on the Mount, Wesley summarized both his own sermon series and Jesus' original sermon by saying, "In a word: let thy religion be the religion of the heart."[5]

When explicating "heart religion" Wesley usually spoke about the "affections" or "tempers" as the true indicators of the nature of the heart. Certainly, what we do says a lot about who we are, as does what we think and to what creeds we give our assent. But Wesley knew that if you want to know who a person truly is, then you have to find out what they love, what they hate, what they take joy in, what they fear, and in what they find peace. If you know these things, you know a person in an unmistakable way. Wesley's view was that if Christianity does not affect a person on this most elemental level, then it has not really taken root.

By preaching and writing about a religion that affects the core of who we are—a religion that reorders the loves and fears of our everyday existence—Wesley knew that he was running very clear risks. But in his mature reflections, which showed a very subtle insight into both human nature and the nature of Christian truth, he did avoid the worst pitfalls that endanger "heart religion." Let us briefly examine three key elements of his understanding of the "religious affections" that helped him avoid some of these pitfalls. I will share here the skeleton of Wesley's understanding without sharing the full documentation in the original sources, which I have presented elsewhere.[6]

First of all, for Wesley the affections or tempers are not the same as "feelings" (understood as a conscious awareness of sensation). Though Wesley sometimes spoke without observing this distinction (especially early in his career), his mature thought reflected this insight. A person can love God (or anyone else, for that matter) without constantly feeling that love. Let us consider a secular, commonsense example to illustrate this distinction.

Just because a mechanic is not feeling love for her husband while she is concentrating on rebuilding a carburetor is no proof that she in fact does not love her husband. Accordingly, defining the religious affections (e.g., humility, love, joy, peace, patience) as the essence of Christianity does not mean that one must be constantly aware of feeling these specific sensations. Having a set of emotions is different from always feeling those emotions. As Wesley said in a letter to Thomas Olivers: "Barely to feel no sin, or to feel constant peace, joy, and love, will not prove the point."[7]

A second crucial feature of Wesley's understanding of heart religion is that the religious affections are transitive, that is, they take objects. The objects that are taken determine, in part, whether the affections are truly religious or not. If what we love is our own lust, or riches, or fame, or flattery, then our affections are focused on things of the "world" or the "flesh." If, on the other hand, what we love is God and our neighbor, if we take joy in the burden of sin being lifted, if it is our walk with God and not our bank account that gives us peace, then our heart is focused on the objects that make for a true "heart religion." In his *Explanatory Notes Upon the New Testament*, Wesley makes this point while commenting on Romans 8:5:

> They that are after the flesh. . . . Mind the things of the flesh—Have their thoughts and affections fixed on such things as gratify corrupt nature: namely, on things visible and temporal; on things of the earth, on plea- sure (of sense or imagination), praise, or riches. But they who are after the Spirit—Who are under His guidance. Mind the things of the Spirit—Think of, rel- ish, love things invisible, eternal; the things which the Spirit hath revealed, which He works in us, moves us to, and promises to give us.[8]

The third key element in Wesley's understanding of the Christian heart is that the affections or emotions dispose us to certain kinds of behavior. If the above-mentioned mechanic tends to place her husband's needs on the same level as her own, if she shares her time and money with him, if his welfare is at least as important as her own, then we might be willing to grant that she in fact loves her husband. But those things (to varying degrees) are all observable; they are a function of her behavior.

Emotions, then, dispose people to behave in certain ways. Just as a glass is, by its nature, disposed to break when it is struck, so a loving person is disposed to act in the perceived best interests of the beloved. The feelings will come and go, but if the behaviors are not there, then true love surely is not. In his fourth discourse on the Sermon on the Mount, Wesley states that while "it is most true that the root of religion lies in the heart," it is also true that such a root "cannot but put forth branches."[9]

These last two points bring out the fact that the religious affections as Wesley understood them are intrinsically relational—in other words, they manifest themselves in our relations with other people and with the world around us. They are, therefore, not secret and unexplainable inward events. If we do not reach beyond ourselves and direct our attention to the God that is depicted in scripture, then we are not growing the truly "religious" affections. For example, if we let the lyrics and images of music videos, instead of the cross of Christ, define for us what "love" means, then what we call "love" will not reflect the biblical understanding. Similarly, if our affections are not strong enough to dispose us to act on them in the social world, then they are not truly "religious." For example, if our compassion for the hungry does not lead us to concrete action in their behalf, then it is not truly Christian compassion. The "religious affections" must break out of the cocoon of individuality at both their birth and their fulfillment in order for Wesley's version of "heart religion" to be fostered and maintained.

These, then, are the formal elements of the "affections of

the heart": they are not the same as feelings, they are generated by focusing our attention on certain objects, and they serve as dispositions or motivations to behave. If we keep these elements in mind, then we can see the intellectual integrity and doctrinal fidelity of Wesley's "orthokardia." In light of Wesley's views about our spiritual/emotional life, a heart religion need not embody the dangers that I named at the beginning of this chapter. Indeed, it has the potential for meeting our deepest hopes for the life of the heart.

Pertinent Sermons of John Wesley

"The Almost Christian" (sermon 2); "The Circumcision of the Heart" (sermon 17); "Upon Our Lord's Sermon on the Mount" Discourses One, Two, Three, and Thirteen (sermons 21–23, and 33).

Wesleyan Hymn on "Heart Religion"

"I Want a Principle Within" (# 410 UMH)

I want a principle within of watchful, godly fear,
a sensibility of sin, a pain to feel it near.
I want the first approach to feel of pride or wrong desire,
to catch the wandering of my will, and quench the kindling fire.

From thee that I no more may stray, no more thy goodness grieve,
grant me the filial awe, I pray, the tender conscience give.
Quick as the apple of an eye, O God, my conscience make;
awake my soul when sin is nigh, and keep it still awake.

Almighty God of truth and love, to me thy power
    impart;
the mountain from my soul remove, the hardness from
    my heart.
O may the least omission pain my reawakened soul,
and drive me to that blood again, which makes the
    wounded whole.

Notes on "I Want a Principle Within"

This originally was titled "For a Tender Conscience" and was first published in 1749.

Verse One: What is a "heart religion" but a "principle within," a clear sense of peace and focus that comes from a well-settled disposition of the heart? What follows may surprise the reader, though. Charles Wesley is asking for a "watchful, godly fear," to be sensitive to sin, especially pride and wrong desire. When many people think of "heart religion" they think of pleasant feelings, but Wesley knew there is more to the picture than that. Fear of sin is one of the foundational elements of this heart religion.

Verse Two: The "filial awe" spoken of here is the respect that a parent is due from a child; it is this respect that will provide a "tender conscience." He then asks not to be spared all possible temptations, but instead asks for vigilance against the sin that he knows will come his way. The phrase the "apple of an eye" refers to the eye's pupil—Wesley is asking that our conscience would be as sensitive to sin as the pupil is to light.

Verse Three: Here he asks for God's power, the power to be made holy that can come only from God. The hardness of his heart is like a mountain that only God can remove. The greatest source of this power is the blood of the crucified Savior, the blood that can make the broken and weak whole and strong—complete and ready joyously to serve the one true God.

See also "Where Shall My Wandering Soul Begin" (# 342 UMH, text only). This is the hymn that Charles most likely wrote just after his conversion.

Suggestions for Further Reading

For biographical information on John Wesley, see *John Wesley* by Stanley Ayling (Nashville: Abingdon, 1979). For a glimpse of some of the many works in the broad stream of writings about the "heart" in the Christian tradition, see the series of abridgments available as a set entitled *Great Devotional Classics* (Nashville, TN: The Upper Room, 1961) and the new series *Upper Room Spiritual Classics* (1997). For an overview of the beginnings of the Methodist movement, see *Wesley and the People Called Methodist* by Richard P. Heitzenrater (Nashville, TN: Abingdon Press, 1995).

Questions for Reflection or Discussion

(Remember—if you are using this book in a small-group setting, all personal conversations should be treated as confidential.)

• What are your fears about "heart religion"? What are your hopes? How do these hopes and fears shape your understanding of the church and its mission? Does the church address your deepest fears and hopes or does it avoid them? How can you help the church engage these deep passions of our hearts?

• How have you seen someone else go astray in the name of "heart religion"? What specifically went wrong? How might this have been avoided?

• What emotions define you? What is it that you truly love? What is it you truly fear? In what do you take your deepest joy? What brings you peace?

Notes

[1] Portions of "John Wesley's Vision of Heart Religion—Ortho-kardia" were previously presented at the American Academy of Religion's "Wesley Studies" working group, 1992 national meeting, and at the 1992 Oxford Institute of Methodist Theological Studies.

[2] See vol. V, sermon 14, "The Repentance of Believers," 343 and Professor Albert C. Outler's note, 343; and sermon 26, "Upon Our Lord's Sermon on the Mount: Discourse the Sixth," 573ff., both in *The Works of John Wesley*, vol. I (Nashville, TN: Abingdon Press, 1985). All references to Wesley's *Works* will be to the Abingdon edition series, edited by Albert C. Outler, unless otherwise indicated.

[3] See my "Orthokardia: The Practical Theology of John Wesley's Heart Religion" in *Quarterly Review* vol. 10, no. 1 (Spring 1990): 49–66, and my *John Wesley on Religious Affections: His Views on Experience and Emotion and their Role in the Christian Life and Theology* (Metuchen: Scarecrow, 1989).

[4] "Sermon on the Mount, I," sermon 21, 481.

[5] *Works*, vol. I, sermon 33, 698. On "heart religion" see Outler's note 134 to sermon 25 ("Sermon on the Mount, V"), *Works*, vol. I, 571, and my works cited above.

[6] See note 3 above.

[7] *Letters*, John Telford, ed., vol. III, 212.

[8] *Explanatory Notes Upon the New Testament* by John Wesley, M.A., London: Charles H. Kelly, 1749), 547.

[9] Wesley's *Works*, vol. I, sermon 24, 541.

Chapter Two

The House of Religion:
The Porch of Repentance

John Wesley's Schematic Diagram of Christianity in a Human Life

 In his "Principles of a Methodist Farther Explained," John Wesley made the following bold declaration: "Our main doctrines, which include all the rest, are three—that of repentance, of faith, and of holiness. The first of these we account, as it were, the porch of religion; the next, the door; the third, religion itself."[1]

At other points in his writings, one can find similar summaries of the fundamental doctrines of Christianity as Wesley understood them. While there are some differences between these various summaries, it is clear that throughout his mature life, he never renounced any of these three doctrines as being foundational for the Christian life.[2] Nowhere else does he provide such a helpful visual image as he does here in this reference to the "house of religion."

While there are shortcomings to having these three key doctrines linked through this image of the house—and I will point out some of these shortcomings later—it is also a powerful and memorable way to summarize the essence of Christianity. Let us now turn to the first part of the image and that aspect of heart religion which Wesley saw as absolutely fundamental for the Christian life: repentance.

The Porch of Repentance

As is true with the concept of "heart religion," people often have ideas of "repentance" that do more harm than good. Very often when people think about repentance, an image of a nagging and judgmental authority figure comes to mind. People often think of being scolded for their sins. They see a dreary vision of God and the Christian life, as though God were a parent who is always telling us to "Stand up straight!" when we would rather slouch. Who would want to claim a "heart religion" that makes us cross such a "porch" seemingly made of upturned rusty nails and splintered wood waiting to pierce our tender feet?

Fortunately, scripture provides us with quite a different understanding of "repentance." It is an understanding that does not crush the human spirit, but instead gives us new life in surprising and powerful ways. Let us consider how Wesley understood the biblical conception of repentance and then look at several specific scriptural texts to see how this repentance is brought about.

Wesley's Understanding of Repentance: Poverty of Spirit and Self-Knowledge

In his thirteen-part series of sermons "Upon Our Lord's Sermon on the Mount," Wesley states that in the fifth chapter of Matthew "Our Lord, first, lays down the sum of all true religion in eight particulars."[3] These "eight particulars" are, of course, the "beatitudes." The first of these is "Blessed are the poor in spirit, for theirs is the kingdom of heaven."

Repentance As "Poverty of Spirit"

In commenting on this first beatitude, Wesley says that "real Christianity always begins in poverty of spirit" and, again,

"The foundation of all is 'poverty of spirit.'" So what does this phrase mean? Wesley says that Jesus was not referring to

> they that are poor as to outward circumstances . . . but the "poor in spirit"; they who, whatever their outward circumstances are, have that disposition of heart which is the first step to all real, substantial happiness, either in this world or that which is to come. . . .
>
> Who then are the poor in spirit? Without question, the humble; they who know themselves, who are convinced of sin; those to whom God hath given that first repentance which is previous to faith in Christ. . . .
>
> [How is the sinner aware of his or her state? The sinner] sees more and more of the evil tempers which spring from that evil root: the pride and haughtiness of spirit, the constant bias to think of himself more highly than he ought to think; the vanity, . . . the hatred or envy, the jealousy or revenge, the anger, malice, or bitterness; the inbred enmity both against God and man which appears in ten thousand shapes; the love of the world, self-will, the foolish and hurtful desires which cleave to his inmost soul. . . . His guilt is now also before his face.
>
> Poverty of spirit, then, . . . "is a just sense of our inward and outward sins, and of our guilt and helplessness."[4]

Repentance As "Self-Knowledge"

Another phrase that was equivalent to meaning "truly repentant" for Wesley was to say that someone had true "self-knowledge." For instance, at the end of his series of sermons on the Sermon on the Mount, Wesley asks the reader to examine on what foundation he or she builds (with reference to Matt. 7:21-27). Wesley asks the reader: Do you expect to enter the kingdom of heaven by orthodoxy (having right ideas)? Or perhaps based on the fact that you do no harm, or perhaps because you are zealous of good works (orthopraxis)? He scoffs at all of this saying,

> Learn to hang naked upon the cross of Christ, counting all thou hast done but dung and dross. Apply to him just in the spirit of the dying thief, of the harlot with her seven devils; else thou art still on the sand, and after saving others thou wilt lose thy own soul.

And how are we to accomplish this? "Now, therefore, build thou upon a rock. By the grace of God, know thyself."[5]

While these two terms—*repentance* and *self-knowledge*—might not seem equivalent to us, Wesley's use of *self-knowledge* offers insight into the human heart: we do not truly know who we are until we confess our sinfulness. Oddly enough, Bob Dylan expressed this truth in one of his lyrics. Bob Dylan, that songwriter-protester of the 1960s and beyond, has been through many twists and turns in his career and his spiritual journey. I do not know how to characterize his own commitment to God at this point, but at one time, he did consider himself a Christian. During that time he produced an album, *Slow Train Coming*, that was filled with Christian imagery. One of those songs, "When He Returns," contains a passage that speaks to this idea of repentance as self-knowledge:

> How long can you falsify and deny what is real?
> How long can you hate yourself for the weakness you
>   conceal?

When we are completely honest with ourselves we cannot help but know that we are not holy, and it is liberating to speak this truth. When we conceal this knowledge, when we suppress it, try to swallow it or sit on it, we feel like a phony. We put on our masks and act as if everything is fine and we have no problems. And what is the result of this? We hate ourselves.

When we repent, instead of denying ourselves, we name the truth of who we are. We name it to God, to the world, and to ourselves. We know that God already knew it (and chances are extremely good that the world around us already knew it!), but when we consciously confess that we are in need of God's help, we free ourselves from the prison of self-hatred that we imposed on ourselves because of our fearful and tragically misguided desire to hide it. When we drop the mask of dishonesty we are taking a step toward a life of faith-filled integrity where the interior life is reflected in the exterior life. We know ourselves, and we repent. Instructive here is one short verse in the story of the prodigal son (a story I will comment on further in this chapter). When the prodigal decided to say no to his old way of life and repent, the Bible says that he "came to himself" (Luke 15:17)—a description of true self-knowledge.

If we now have a sense of what Wesley meant when he spoke about "repentance," let us move on to the practical question of how this repentance is to be brought about in human hearts. For this task we will see how repentance is brought about in three Bible stories.

How Repentance Is Brought About

Isaiah 6:1-5

Chapter 6 of the book of Isaiah records Isaiah's call to his role as prophet. Any familiarity people have with this passage usually stems from Isaiah's answer to God's call: "Here am I; send me" (v. 10). Isaiah's response is often held up as a model of obedience to the call of God. What is important for our concern with repentance, however, are the first few verses that relate Isaiah's initial encounter with God. These read as follows:

In the year that King Uzziah died, I saw the Lord sitting on a throne, high and lofty; and the hem of his robe filled the temple. Seraphs were in attendance above him; each had six wings: with two they covered their faces, and with two they covered their feet, and with two they flew. And one called to another and said:

"Holy, holy holy is the LORD of hosts;
the whole earth is full of his glory."

The pivots on the thresholds shook at the voices of those who called, and the house filled with smoke. And I said: "Woe is me! I am lost, for I am a man of unclean lips, and I live among a people of unclean lips; yet my eyes have seen the King, the Lord of hosts!"

Isaiah is given a fleeting glimpse of God, and the angelic seraphs put the experience into words by announcing that God is holy and the earth is full of his glory. What is Isaiah's response to this confrontation with God's presence, a presence best described as "holy" and filling the earth with his "glory"? The first words out of Isaiah's mouth are "Woe is me! I am lost, for I am a man of unclean lips, and I live among a people of unclean lips; yet my eyes have seen the King, the LORD of hosts!" (v. 5). In other words, almost simultaneous with Isaiah's awareness of the holiness of God is his awareness of his own sinfulness.

This is a pattern found throughout scripture, yet so often overlooked by people trying to walk the Christian life: repentance—the awareness of and sorrow for our sinfulness, our awareness that we are not the creature that God created us to be—comes most powerfully when we are confronted with God's holiness. You will notice that it was not somebody nagging at Isaiah about how bad he was that brought him to a confession of his "lostness"; it was seeing God, and immediately being aware that, compared to God, we are unclean.

"Woe is me!" Confronting holiness brings true and deep repentance. Our next scriptural example of this phenomenon comes from the New Testament.

Luke 5:1-11

In the beginning of Luke 5, Jesus gets into Simon's boat, pushes off a little way from shore, and then teaches the crowds of people who are gathered on the banks (see verse 3). The passage then continues:

> When he had finished speaking, he said to Simon, "Put out into the deep water and let down your nets for a catch." Simon answered, "Master, we have worked all night long but have caught nothing. Yet if you say so, I will let down the nets." When they had done this, they caught so many fish that their nets were beginning to break. So they signaled their partners in the other boat to come and help them. And they came and filled both boats, so that they began to sink. But when Simon Peter saw it, he fell down at Jesus' knees, saying, "Go away from me, Lord, for I am a sinful man!" For he and all who were with him were amazed at the catch of fish that they had taken.

Simon Peter utters the simple statement that is definitive of true repentance: "I am a sinful man!" He does this not because someone has scolded him about his behavior, but because he has confronted true holiness in the miraculous catch of fish. He says to Jesus: "Go away from me, Lord." Being in the presence of one who could work such a miracle—one so holy—was painful for Simon Peter because it showed him so clearly what he was not. Yet Peter was not left stammering and cowering. Like Isaiah before him, out of the midst of his sense of unworthiness he was called into a life of service to the Holy One:

Then Jesus said to Simon, "Do not be afraid; from now on you will be catching people." When they had brought their boats to shore, they left everything and followed him.

Also like Isaiah before him, Peter's personal self-judgment was elicited by the holiness of God. This pattern can be seen in another passage in Luke's Gospel.

Luke 15:11-32

In Luke 15 we have what is sometimes called the "Bible's lost-and-found." The chapter begins with the parable of the lost sheep, continues with the parable of the lost coin, and concludes with the parable of the lost son (sometimes called the "prodigal" son because of his wild excesses). This last parable, perhaps one of the most famous stories in the entire Bible, contains the memorable repentance of the son who lived a life of dissipation only in the end to come home and be reconciled with his father. For our purposes, the key verses are 20 and 21 that describe his return home:

> So he set off and went to his father. But while he was still far off, his father saw him and was filled with compassion; he ran and put his arms around him and kissed him. Then the son said to him, "Father, I have sinned against heaven and before you; I am no longer worthy to be called your son."

The son had come home seeking employment as a mere hired hand in his father's estate. He was broken and disheartened by his pursuit of the world's empty pleasures. But it was only in the forgiving embrace of his father—offered before any words were uttered—that he could confess his sinfulness. After the father embraces him, verse 21 begins, "*Then* the son said to him, "Father, I have sinned..." (emphasis mine). Confronted by the holiness of his father's unconditional love and forgiveness, the prodigal son is free to speak of his sinfulness, he is free to repent.

"I Surrender"

The same dynamic that is seen in these scripture passages is also beautifully conveyed in the lyrics of a contemporary Christian song titled "I Surrender." Surrender is usually associated with the grim realities of war, the degradation of denying who you want to be and unwillingly taking on a new identity—that of prisoner. This song, however, beautifully puts the word in a Christian context:

> To Your majesty
> And your beauty
> I surrender.
> To your holiness
> And your love
> I surrender
> For You are an awesome God
> Who is mighty
> You deserve my deepest praise
> With all of my heart
> And all of my life
> I surrender

It is not to the nagging or judging of some moralistic nanny-God that the singer surrenders, but to God's beauty, majesty, love, and holiness. Nothing could convey so clearly the nature of true repentance.

The student of scripture might say at this point: "What about stories like Nathan's confronting David? Is not that an example of someone coming to repent because they are confronted by their sinfulness?" Similarly, those who know Wesley's career know that he often "preached the law" to people until they repented. Do these examples not contradict our paradigm that repentance results from an encounter with holiness? No.

For both the prophet Nathan and for John Wesley, to confront people with the law of God is to confront them with the holiness of God. It was only after David was invited to consider the law of God by being asked to judge a fictitious case that he named his own sinfulness (2 Samuel 12:1-13). And when we read Wesley's sermon explaining the law, we see that one of the most basic defining characteristics of God's law is that it is holy.[6] On this point we can also look to the Old Testament prophets' constant desire to bring repentance, not judgment. (Which is not to say that sometimes we sinful humans would prefer, unfortunately, the destruction of our enemies rather than their repentance. See the book of Jonah for an example of such an attitude.)

None of this detracts from our basic principle that pointing people to their sins can only bring guilt, while pointing them to God brings a genuine awareness of their sinfulness. David, like the nominal Christians in Wesley's time, had agreed to be accountable for a certain standard of behavior in light of God's commitment to him. To point out to someone that they have not lived up to their commitment is a sad but necessary part of the Christian life. But when done in the right spirit, it does not make the fallen persons focus on their sins but instead directs them to the holiness of God.

Repentance and the Distinction between Sin and Sins

Very often when people think in a general way about what "being religious" means, they will think of something along the lines of the abstract, parental-sounding command: "Be good." This "being good" is usually further specified by a series of actions such as going to church, saying your prayers at night, giving a tithe, and so forth. *Not* being "religious," on the other hand, is usually described in terms of "bad acts"—sins (in the plural). But repentance as we have seen it described by Wesley and in 2 Samuel 12 quoted above is something much deeper and more fundamental to the human heart than recognizing our bad acts. In the biblical sense of repentance, when we repent, we repent from sin—a state of being out of relationship with God. The plural term *sins* refers to the acts that flow out of our ruptured relationship with God, which in turn is described by the singular word *sin*. The difference between these two can be illustrated by a visual image.

Imagine you are walking down a path when suddenly you stumble over a branch. You say "Oops," regain your balance, and continue on your way. Many people will think that saying this kind of "oops" after stumbling is what repentance is all about, but they are thinking about sin in the wrong way. When we confront the holiness of God, it is not like stumbling over a branch and continuing on our same path. When we confront the holiness of God—and in so doing confront our sinfulness— we turn from the path we were walking and choose to walk in an entirely new direction. In fact, the original Hebrew and Greek words in the Bible that are translated *repentance* literally refer to turning and changing one's mind.

This repentance is not just saying "Sorry!" every time we commit some particular sin. It means turning away from the way that leads to death and seeking a restored relationship with God—turning from sin to God. This turning from sin obviously has implications for our sins (and I will return to that topic in chapter 4 on holiness), but what is important for our purposes here is to see that repentance is first and foremost about our fundamental relationship with God. Sin is about *being*—who we are in our heart—while sins are about *doing*— the actions that define us in the world. Sin is the cause, sins are the effect, and repentance is about rooting out the cause.

A Stumbling Block: Sin As Pride

Classically, sin has been understood as pride, worshiping one-self as God. It seems a laughable image when stated that bluntly; but in fact, people do tend to worship themselves even if they would not use that language. They act as if they are the ones who created the rules, that they are the ones who make all of the important decisions about their lives, that they decide what is going on. To live this way is to live as if there is no God but you.

In some of the retreats that I have led, some people have objected to this characterization of sin as pride. A few of them have said that pride does not always describe their experience of sin. Some have said that more typically their greatest sin is the opposite of pride; it is the tendency to value oneself too lowly, to have no self-esteem. These people have said that to describe sin in terms of pride is to take away what little self-esteem they have; it seems to grind them down further into the dust of their own self-hatred and reinforces what the world has already done to them. I value this testimony of real-life experience, but I would evaluate it in a slightly different way.

Some will take their own self-assessment based on their feelings about themselves and say that they are in charge of their own domain and the only one who has to be pleased, while others will consult their own feelings and see themselves as helpless and weak or even as worthless and downtrodden. But the problem with both of these scenarios is that in each case, the people have taken *their own* assessment of themselves as being definitive. Here are two different people, making two quite opposite assessments of themselves. Yet we could describe *both* as committing the sin of pride because in each case they are relying on their own self-assessment as the source of ultimate truth.

To take one's "experience" on this issue as authoritative without question—whether that experience says you are the center of the universe or whether it says you are worthless—is wrong. Our experience always needs to be judged by the Word that comes to us from outside of us, the Word that we did not create. Some people might say that their feelings came "naturally," that they came by them honestly and never consciously decided to feel this way. We have no reason to doubt this statement. In fact, that is why we call sin universal—it can take many forms, infect all parts of our experience, and seem "normal." But that does not mean that it is right. It is better to say that these vastly different self-assessments into which people are invited by our culture come unconsciously. Once we raise them up to the surface of our consciousness, however, we can offer them up for judgment and correction by God's loving, transforming Holy Spirit. Taking our own experience as definitive, no matter the nature of that experience, is a species of pride that denies the Lord's place as judge over us.

The good news comes as a proclamation from outside of us; it is not found as some "depth dimension" within us that we can stumble onto after enough rummaging around in our souls. The problem with some contemporary "spirituality" is that it never diverts the eyes and ears away from the self long enough for a person to see and hear the gospel proclaimed. While even the word of God comes to us with cultural trappings, the Christian trusts that with the Holy Spirit leading us, the community can discern God's word when we humbly seek it.

And what *does* the word of God say about who we are as human beings? The Bible says that we are created in the image of God, that God created us male and female, and that we are a good creation. But the Bible also says that all of us have fallen into sin, that we are not the creatures that God created us to be (see Genesis 1–4). It is this realization, and the desire to turn from self-centered sin toward God, that describes true repentance.

Two Counterfeits of Repentance

When people become obsessed with their own sins, they actually can avoid true repentance. Instead, they become caught up in two common counterfeits of repentance: remorse and regret. Now *remorse* and *regret* can be used to describe sincere emotions felt by good Christians, but they also can represent a spiritual attitude that undercuts true repentance. A comment that a colleague of mine once made about his home country describes what I mean.

While I was lecturing in a Scandinavian country, a native faculty member said that the dominant spiritual orientation of his fellow citizens is one of "remorse and regret." By this he meant their perpetual state of being downcast, if not morose, and obsessed with one's failures and sinfulness. While such an attitude might seem like a version of being repentant, it instead prevents true repentance.

Those whose attitudes are defined by regret and remorse in this sense have focused their hearts and minds on their own sins and have simply let their attention become fixed on sinfulness. They are no longer focused on the holiness that brings true awareness of their need to change. It is as if they are driving a car that needs to be washed, and they are always thinking about the dirt on the car, but they never take it to the car wash. In this example, having a constant awareness of the dirt—and deep feelings of guilt about it—is seen as a kind of acceptable substitute for washing the car. When put in those terms, such an attitude is laughable, but, unfortunately, it is all too common.[7]

True repentance brings about not only a deep awareness of sin, it brings with it also a burning desire to change, to become more like the holiness that brought us to our knees. That is why Wesley's "porch of repentance" leads directly to the "door of faith" and hence into the "house of holiness." Repentance is oriented toward the future while remorse and regret are past-oriented. Remorse and regret nurse our old failures as if they were sick children when in fact they are bloodsucking parasites and imposters. Remorse and regret rob us of any chance for real change in the present by causing us to obsess over the past. We must leave behind these destructive tendencies if we are to walk into the house of holiness.

Encountering Holiness Today

Let us now consider a basic question that arises in light of what we have seen about repentance: How does one encounter the holiness of God today? If we are to repent from sin and come back to a restored relationship with God, where are we to look for the holiness that transforms hearts?

We have already given one answer by looking at stories from scripture. They convey God's holiness in a special way. But while reading the Bible is a basic and foundational method for encountering God, it is not the only one.

The story we read from Isaiah is quite a special one, recording a vision that few of us are likely to have this side of eternity, with seraphs and smoke and voices.[8] If that is to be the typical way that people encounter God's holiness then most of us (who do not report such experiences) are doomed to go without such repentance-generating encounters. But look at the story of the calling of Peter in Luke 5:1-11. What was the medium for Peter's awareness of the holiness of Jesus? It was nothing more exalted than a net full of fish (v. 6). Or consider the prodigal son: it was the hug of his father that allowed him to speak of his sinfulness (Luke 15:20-21).

Seeing a net full of fish or receiving a father's embrace are experiences that had been encountered before, but the timing and the circumstances made them occasions for these average people to encounter the Holy One in their lives. Such everyday events can be occasions for our encountering God, if we look for God in them, that is, if we have "eyes to see and ears to hear," as Jesus often said. Chapter 5 will deal more specifically with the tools that God has given us for developing the spiritual life, but we need to emphasize here that God can and will use almost anything to reveal God's self if we are open to, and looking for, the Holy One. God is revealed more often to the committed than to the merely curious.

A Final Word of Comfort and Preparation

One final, important point needs to be made about the awareness of our sinfulness that comes from true repentance. When we are confronted by God's holiness, our awareness of our sinfulness can be so overwhelming that our human spirit can seem as though it is about to be crushed completely. When this happens we need to remember that being confronted with our sinfulness is like having light shine into a dusty room: Suddenly we become aware of just how dusty the room is. The realization can be overwhelming. Instantly we see not just the dust on tabletops and chairs, but in full light we see that the very air we have been breathing is full of dust motes: it is everywhere! What a mess!

In such times we need to remember that the light did not actually increase the amount of dust, but only showed the extent of it. The light points out the dust that is already present, but, thankfully, the light also shows us what to do next. That brings us to the next step in our spiritual journey: the door of faith.

Pertinent Sermons of John Wesley

"The Scripture Way of Salvation" (sermon 43) is one of the best summaries of Wesley's theology. On sin, see "Original Sin" (sermon 44) and "The Great Privilege of those that are Born of God" (sermon 19, esp. p. 436). "The Mystery of Iniquity" (sermon 61) provides a commentary on how sin has been an ongoing feature of human history. On the holiness of the law, see "The Original, Nature, Properties, and Use of the Law" (sermon 34). On repentance as self-knowledge, see "The Repentance of Believers" (sermon 14). This same sermon also discusses the repentance that is to be a continual part of our lives.

Wesleyan Hymn on Repentance

"Depth of Mercy" (# 355 UMH)

Depth of mercy! Can there be
mercy still reserved for me?
Can my God his wrath forbear,
me, the chief of sinners, spare?

I have long withstood his grace,
long provoked him to his face,
would not hearken to his calls,
grieved him by a thousand falls.

I my Master have denied,
I afresh have crucified,
oft profaned his hallowed name,
put him to an open shame.

There for me the Savior stands,
shows his wounds and spreads his hands.
God is love! I know, I feel;
Jesus weeps and loves me still.

Now incline me to repent,
let me now my sins lament,
now my foul revolt deplore,
weep, believe, and sin no more.

Notes on "Depth of Mercy"

This was written in 1740 and was originally titled "After a Relapse into Sin." In the 1780 collection of hymns that the Wesleys put together, this was the first hymn in the section titled "For Mourners Convinced of Backsliding." This original title and section heading show the continual need for our repentance. Wesley never saw repentance as a one-time experience but as part of the ongoing Christian way of life.

Verse One: Can there really be mercy for someone like me when it is clear what a sinner I am? At the end, we see a very typical sentiment of the penitent expressed—that no one could be a worse sinner than me. In a sense this is always true, for our sinfulness puts us equidistant from God: All of us are completely separated from God, except for the grace-filled reaching out from God through Jesus. "Chief of sinners" is a reference to 1 Timothy 1:15.

Verse Two: We might not have known it until after our confrontation with holiness, but in the light of that holiness, we can look back on our lives and name numerous times when we "withstood his grace" and "provoked him to his face."

Verse Three: "I my Master have denied." If "Master" conjures images of the cruelty of American slavery, then it is not helpful. Wesley used it, however, to emphasize the sovereignty of God that lovingly calls us into submission. Our own sins crucifying Jesus anew is a reference to Hebrews 6:6.

Verse Four: The Savior's wounds show that God is love. Not only this, but I know that Jesus loves me. This is not an abstract knowledge of God in general, but God in relation to my particular sins. I am still loved in spite of the sin that I now see as present in my life!

Verse Five: "Now incline me to repent" the sinner asks for help even in repenting—we are dependent on God at all stages in our journey. The very end of this verse is a kind of microcosm of the entire house of religion: "weep"—the porch of repentance; "believe"—the door of faith; and "sin no more"—holiness.

See also "Just as I Am, Without One Plea," # 357 (UMH). This is not a Wesleyan hymn but is perhaps the classic hymn that conveys the heart of the repentant person. Note the absolute self-knowledge that is implied in that simple but powerful phrase "Just as I am"—a striking illustration of a Wesleyan understanding of repentance as "self-knowledge." For another Wesleyan hymn on repentance see # 417 (UMH), "O For a Heart to Praise My God."

Suggestions for Further Reading

The outstanding classic, not only regarding repentance and humility but the whole spiritual life in general, is Thomas à Kempis's *The Imitation of Christ*. Wesley constantly recommended this book as a key resource for spiritual growth. The homily "On Admonition and Repentance" by Ephraim Syrus (306-377 C.E.), one of the early church fathers and a writer whom Wesley greatly admired and recommended to others, is instructive on repentance. At the very beginning of this homily, Ephraim says: "Not of compulsion is the doctrine; of free-will is the word of life." What a pithy summary of the repentance we find in the presence of holiness as opposed to the moralistic "repentance" that is dragged out of us through judgmental attitudes. *Nicene and Post-Nicene Fathers*, Second Series, vol. 13, 330.

Questions for Reflection or Discussion

Remember a time when you nagged someone, trying to use moralistic arguments to bring that person to repentance. What happened in your relationship with that person? How did it affect that person's relationship with God? Did anyone ever use such nagging to try to bring you to repentance? What was its effect?

• When were you ever confronted with holiness in your life? What was the effect of this encounter? How do you go about encountering the holy in the everyday and the ordinary?

• When faced with God's holiness, from what specifically do you feel called to repent? Is this something from which you previously have tried to turn away? How can your repentance be different this time?

• If you are reading this book as part of a small-group study experience, how have other group members held you accountable? How do you help others remain accountable?

• Have you ever tried to be the occasion for someone else to encounter God's holiness? For instance, have you ever really forgiven someone? Have you ever loved someone completely and unconditionally and expressed that love to them? If so, you have been an icon for God's holiness in the world. Be humble and give thanks.

Notes

1 Wesley's *Works*, vol. VIII, 1872 ed., Zondervan Publishing Co., 472.

2 See Richard P. Heitzenrater's *Wesley and the People Called Methodists* (Nashville, TN: Abingdon Press, 1995) where he refers to Wesley's "house" image as containing the "grand doctrines" of Methodism, 156, 204, 215, 242. Albert Outler, the great Wesley scholar, also made regular reference to Wesley's house as a summary of what was important theologically. See Outler's collected works, *The Albert Outler Library* (Anderson, IN: Bristol, 1995), vol. 1, 258ff.; vol. 2, 240ff.; vol. 3, 422–447. See also "Justification by Faith," sermon 5, 197, Outler's note number 93 for Wesley's habitual linking of repentance with faith.

3 *The Works of John Wesley* (Nashville: Abingdon Press, 1984), vol. I, sermon 21, "Upon Our Lord's Sermon on the Mount, Discourse the First," 475.

4 Sermon 21, 475–476, 477–479.

5 "Sermon on the Mount, vol. XIII," sermon 33, 695–696.

6 "Original, Nature, Properties, and Use of the Law," sermon 34.

7 See Jean-Paul Sartre's *The Emotions: Outline of a Theory* (Secaucus, NJ: Carol Publishing Group, 1984), where he speaks about emotions as a kind of failure behavior. That is, when we do not make changes in reality, we can pretend to have done something by feeling something. This kind of attitude is best given the name "sentimentality"—an obsession with our sentiments as opposed to being involved in the social, interpersonal reality where God calls us to be.

8 Another example of this kind of dramatic God-human encounter that brings about repentance is found in Job 38–42. There, after Job has been questioning, challenging, and berating God, he is finally confronted directly by God. Job's response is "My ears had heard of you but now my eyes have seen you. Therefore I despise myself and repent in dust and ashes" (42:5-6, NIV).

Chapter Three

The House of Religion:
The Door of Faith

 Faith is certainly a word that is heard often in discussions of religion, and it can take on several meanings. For our purposes, though, we will focus on two meanings of the term. These two meanings of "faith" are distinguishable from each other, yet they are closely related. In order to make clear the distinction, let me share with you a story that a student once told me.

There was a tightrope walker who had just walked across a dangerous gorge with the aid of the long pole that people in his profession use for balance. After completing the walk, he asked the crowd if they thought he could do it again, only this time pushing a wheelbarrow in front of him for balance. Some doubted it, some believed him. He proved the doubters wrong, however, when he completed the walk while pushing the wheelbarrow. He then asked if the people thought that he could push the wheelbarrow across the rope with a person sitting inside of the wheelbarrow. Having seen him twice prove his prowess for them, the people all shouted out that they believed he could do so. Their eager encouragement turned to stony silence, though, when he asked which one of them would be the first to take the ride.

Therein lies the two meanings of faith that I want to explore in this chapter. It is one thing to state that you believe—have faith—that such and so is the case. It is another thing to stake your life on it. To use a term from the last chapter, faith in this sense is a question of deciding to whom you are going to surrender.

Two Understandings of "Faith" or "Belief"

Faith—and its closely related term *belief*—can mean either the doctrines that describe the essential core of a religion or it can mean simply "trust." In the first sense of the word, we might hear someone refer to "the Christian faith" or "Christian beliefs" and mean by that a collection of such statements as "Jesus was God incarnate," "Jesus died for the sins of the world," or "Jesus was raised from the dead." Sometimes these statements are gathered into a compact summary statement of the important things about the Christian life that need to find a home in the life of a believer. These are called "creeds" from the Latin word *credo* which means "I believe." These gospel summaries have been a part of Christianity since the very beginning.

Peter's sermon in Acts 10:34-43 is one of the earliest collections of the basic components of the Christian "faith." He recounts the preparatory ministry of John the Baptist, how Jesus was anointed with the Holy Spirit, how he performed healings, was crucified, was raised on the third day, appeared to the apostles, and commanded them to preach the good news to the people. Interestingly enough, at the end of his recitation of this creedlike declaration of what God has done in Christ, Peter uses *believe* in the second sense of the term, that is, as meaning "trust."

In verse 43, Peter says of Jesus that "All the prophets testify about him that everyone who *believes* in him receives forgiveness of sins through his name" (emphasis mine). Here the sense of *believe* is clearly trust: all those who trust in him will receive forgiveness of their sins. A friend and colleague once told me that in a West African language, the word for faith literally means "You can rest your weight on it." This beautifully describes this understanding of faith.

The fact that belief-as-doctrine and belief-as-trust are linked here is no coincidence. When one analyzes these two different understandings, it becomes apparent immediately that neither one of these senses of *faith* or *belief* could stand alone as adequately describing a religious life. A person could, for instance, memorize all of the classical creeds of the church—such as the Apostles' Creed, the Nicene Creed, and the Athanasian Creed—and have a tremendous intellectual grasp on all of the doctrines of the "faith," and yet have a life that looks nothing like what a Christian life should be. John Wesley called this kind of faith a "cold, lifeless assent, a train of ideas in the head."[1] Wesley went on to say that without faith as a "disposition of the heart"—that is, trust—the intellectual assent had no saving power. But the opposite is also true.

If one were to try to live religiously by faith-as-trust alone, the immediate question would be: "All right, whom or what do you trust?" This question points to the "transitive" nature of trust.[2] Trust, like all of the "religious affections," is transitive: it takes an object. To say "I trust . . ." leaves people asking, "What?" What is the object of your trust? The object of our trust as Christians is the God revealed in Christ, the God whose actions are described by our creeds, that is, the God who forgives sins, gives eternal life, raises from the dead. Just as faith-as-assent-to-doctrine cannot stand alone, neither can faith-as-trust; they need each other. This can be seen in a quote from Wesley's sermon "Salvation by Faith": "What faith is it then through which we are saved? It may be answered: first, in general, it is a faith in Christ—Christ, and God through Christ, are the proper object of it."[3]

This faith is best exemplified in scripture by Ephesians 2:8-9 and Hebrews 11. Ephesians 2:8-9 reads: "For by grace you have been saved through faith, and this is not your own doing;

it is the gift of God—not the result of works, so that no one may boast." Wesley referred time and again to Hebrews 11:1 when giving a concise summary of faith. It reads: "Now faith is the assurance of things hoped for, the conviction of things not seen." But this faith that comes as a gift of grace—this faith that is both assurance and conviction—is finally not just a general trust in the God of the Bible. The faith that is the door of Wesley's "house of religion" is, at its heart, the specific faith that our sins are forgiven and our broken relationship with God is healed.

The Substance of Our Faith: Christ's Work Has Brought about Our Forgiveness

The center of virtually every local church's worship space contains a cross. Crosses can be found in a seemingly endless variety of appearance: some are small and made of metal, some are large and made of wood, while others are depicted in stained glass. But regardless of appearance, the cross typically stands at the center of the worship space. It stands there—and is the most recognizable symbol in all of Christianity—because it stands at the center of our faith. On the cross, that cruel form of execution used by the ruling Romans in first-century Palestine, Jesus died a death that made him the savior of the world. Let us consider a few texts from the Bible that speak to this point.

Hebrews 9 contains what is perhaps the classic statement on the death of Christ and the forgiveness of sin. The author of Hebrews says that when Christ came as a high priest he entered into the Holy Place of the temple "not with the blood of goats and calves, but with his own blood, thus obtaining eternal redemption" (v. 12). His sacrifice was necessary because "without the shedding of blood there is no forgiveness of sins" (v. 22). This statement is recapitulated in verses 26-28 where the author says:

He has appeared once for all at the end of the age to remove sin by the sacrifice of himself. And just as it is appointed for mortals to die once, and after that the judgment, so Christ, having been offered once to bear the sins of many, will appear a second time, not to deal with sin, but to save those who are eagerly waiting for him.

In Colossians 1, we read that God the Father is to be thanked because "He has rescued us from the power of darkness and transferred us into the kingdom of his beloved Son, in whom we have redemption, the forgiveness of sins" (vv. 13-14). Later in this same chapter we see more explicitly how this redemption came about: "For in [Jesus Christ] all the fullness of God was pleased to dwell, and through him God was pleased to reconcile to himself all things, whether on earth or in heaven, by making peace through the blood of his cross" (vv. 19-20).

Apostle Paul in Galatians 3:13-14 says that "Christ redeemed us from the curse of the law by becoming a curse for us—for it is written, 'Cursed is everyone who hangs on a tree'—in order that in Christ Jesus the blessing of Abraham might come to the Gentiles, so that we might receive the promise of the Spirit through faith." Ephesians 1:7-10 reinforces this theme when it proclaims that:

In him we have redemption through his blood, the forgiveness of our trespasses, according to the riches of his grace that he lavished on us. With all wisdom and insight he has made known to us the mystery of his will, according to his good pleasure that he set forth in Christ, as a plan for the fullness of time, to gather up all things in him, things in heaven and things on earth.

Later in that same book, Ephesians 4:31-32, we see this central act of forgiveness used as a motivation for our own behavior:

> Put away from you all bitterness and wrath and anger and wrangling and slander, together with all malice, and be kind to one another, tenderhearted, forgiving one another, as God in Christ has forgiven you.

The references could go on and on, but the point is clear: The death of Jesus on the cross has brought about the forgiveness of sins. All can have access to this forgiveness if they have faith—that is, if they trust that God has in fact worked in the cross and resurrection of Christ to forgive our sins. This pivotal point in the believer's journey with God is called *justification* by theologians—or the awareness of the forgiveness of our sins by God. John Wesley put it this way:

> The plain scriptural notion of justification is pardon, the forgiveness of sins. It is that act of God the Father whereby, for the sake of the propitiation made by the blood of his Son, he showeth forth his righteousness (or mercy) by the remission of the sins that are past.[4]

If you remember our distinction between "sin" and "sins" you might well ask: "Which is forgiven in the cross of Christ?" The joyful answer is "Both!" The Bible does in fact at different places refer to both the singular "sin" and the plural "sins." Both our wrong relationship with God—our desire to take our own self-assessments as definitive, to put ourselves on the thrones of our hearts—and the sinful actions that flow from that rebelliousness, are forgiven in the perfect saving work of Jesus.

From the Porch to the Door

To accept forgiveness we have to be able to say we need forgiving, and that is why the "porch of repentance" stands in front of the "door of faith." When we are caught up in the worldly way of life where we have to grasp and clutch and defend our self-identity, where we have to maintain the facade of innocence if we are not going to be "put down" by our peers, it does not come naturally to speak of our sins. But when, in humility, we can name our sinfulness in the face of holiness, we no longer have to scratch and bite to defend the pitiful little self-images that we have clawed out of the world. We are given a whole new identity, and it comes completely free: We are forgiven sinners! We are redeemed! It is only after crossing that porch, though, that we are in a position, spiritually speaking, to receive that gift because only then can we trust in Christ's redemption.

The "door of faith," then, is marked with the sign of the cross, and it is only reachable from the porch of repentance. Furthermore, it is only by going through this specific door of the forgiveness of sins that we gain access to the house of holiness. Before we move on to consideration of that house itself, though, let us consider one of the features of this "door of faith" that many people find most troubling.

The Forgiveness of Sin As a Mystery

How could the death of a man on a cross two thousand years ago bring about my forgiveness today? Though the scriptures mentioned in the section "The Substance of Our Faith" are very clear in making this proclamation of forgiveness, no passage in scripture gives an exhaustive explanation of *how* Jesus could "become our sin" and die an atoning death. Theologians have written many books trying to shed light on this fundamental tenet of Christian faith, and they have used several different metaphors,[5] but in the end it must be named what it really is: a mystery.

The most common way that we encounter the term *mystery* in our culture today—namely, in the popular books and movies that go by the literary genre "mystery"—does not help us understand the term in its truest theological sense. "Mystery stories" invite the reader to guess the outcome ahead of time, and if one is clever enough, it can be done. Solving these "mysteries" becomes an intellectual challenge, and even something to compete over: "Oh, I knew who killed the Baron after the third chapter. Hadn't you guessed it by then?"

Real mystery is not like that. A true mystery in the classical theological sense is not something that depends solely on intellectual ability. A true mystery is one that will not yield to any explanation. There are some questions that will never receive satisfying answers this side of heaven. Such mysteries bring us to our knees, literally and spiritually. Real mystery comes as a proclamation, a revelation, and says to us "deal with this." The forgiveness of sins by the death of Jesus on the cross is perhaps the central mystery of the Christian faith.

When confronted by the mystery of how the death of Jesus on the cross two thousand years ago brought about the forgiveness of our sins, our basic approach should not be to try to deny this mystery. Instead we should point out—no, proclaim—the inescapability of mystery in all of life, no matter if one tries to live as a Christian or not. Regardless of what philosophy or theology we use to orient our lives, there is mystery all around us. The question in life is not "How can I avoid mystery?" but is instead "By what mystery will I choose to live?"

Some of the students I have taught over the years have bridled at talk of "mystery." Some say, "I don't want all of that mumbo jumbo about 'mystery.' I am going to stick with what I can taste, feel, smell, see, and hear. That is what is real." In fact, what is so obviously "real" to the eighteen-year-old freshman is fraught with mystery, too, though it often is not named as such.

Many of these freshmen, like many people of all ages in

our culture, are caught up in the pursuit of the things of the five senses. Such people disdain obvious "religious mysteries" in favor of the "hard facts" of science, and the "real world" of business, and our culture's definition of "success" as material-ism, sex, and drugs. But even in the most worldly life where the satisfaction of all bodily appetites is the only apparent value, there is deep mystery.

For instance, if pleasure is so important, why is it not per-manent? Why is it in fact elusive and, when finally achieved, fleeting? Why do the pleasures of sex sometimes lead to disease and death? Why do the pleasures of eating so often lead to obe-sity and the degradation of our health? If wealth is the goal, why is it that only a few can achieve it? These questions reflect features of our reality, yet they seldom are put so bluntly and labeled as "mysteries." But we need to do just such labeling if we are to see that the simple fact of mystery should not turn us away from a Christian perspective. All of life contains myster-ies, and we must choose which mysteries are going to define who we are.

Christians choose the mysterious and wonder-filled life in whose center is the forgiveness of our sins. A whole way of life surrounds this proclamation of the forgiveness of sins; it can be seen in people who are defined by the humility of repentance, the joy and peace that come from knowing that one is forgiven, and hearts that are filled with love. All of the "fruit of the Spirit" mentioned in Galatians 5:22-24 that I will describe in the next chapter grow from that "tree" that we call the cross of Christ. Our trust in that mystery of the forgiveness of sin on the cross of Christ is the true door into the house of holiness.

Trying to "solve" or "answer" or "explain" this mystery is an irrelevant task when you are busy eating of the fruit that grows from this mystery. This is the point made in Charles Wesley's "And Can It Be that I Should Gain" in verse two: " 'Tis mystery all: th'Immortal dies! Who can explore his strange design? . . . let angel minds inquire no more." No, we are not called to explain it. We are called to live it, and proclaim it.

Indeed God is mysterious, whether we encounter God on the cross of Christ or in such direct, repentance-inducing encounters as the ones that Isaiah and Peter experienced. In the end, it is not this mystery that keeps us from God. The mystery is in fact part of what draws us to God.

Repentance, and faith in the forgiveness of our sinfulness, together free us from sin. We no longer have to carry that tremendous burden around on our backs. We can stand up straight and spend our energy on things other than dealing with our sinfulness. But for what are we freed? On what should we be spending all of our newfound energy once we realize that we are forgiven? The answer is that we are freed for—and called into—a life of holiness. Explaining what that means is the next chapter's task.

Pertinent Sermons of John Wesley

For more on the faith that we are forgiven see "Salvation by Faith" (sermon 1); "The New Birth" (sermon 45); and "Justification by Faith" (sermon 5). On how faith is the foundation for everything in the spiritual life see "On Faith (Heb. 11:6)" (sermon 106); "On the Discoveries of Faith" (sermon 117); and "On Faith" (sermon 132).

Wesleyan Hymn on Faith

"And Can It Be that I Should Gain" (# 363 UMH)

> And can it be that I should gain
> an interest in the Savior's blood!
> Died he for me? who caused his pain!
> For me? who him to death pursued?

Amazing love! How can it be
that thou, my God, shouldst die for me?

'Tis mystery all: th'Immortal dies!
Who can explore his strange design?
In vain the first-born seraph tries
to sound the depths of love divine.
'Tis mercy all! Let earth adore;
let angel minds inquire no more.

He left his Father's throne above
(so free, so infinite his grace!),
emptied himself of all but love,
and bled for Adam's helpless race.
'Tis mercy all, immense and free,
for O my God, it found out me!

Long my imprisoned spirit lay,
fast bound in sin and nature's night;
thine eye diffused a quickening ray;
I woke, the dungeon flamed with light;
my chains fell off, my heart was free,
I rose, went forth, and followed thee.

No condemnation now I dread;
Jesus, and all in him, is mine;
alive in him, my living Head,
and clothed in righteousness divine,
bold I approach th'eternal throne,
and claim the crown, through Christ my own.

Notes on "And Can It Be that I Should Gain"

This is one of two hymns that Charles Wesley wrote at the time
of his conversion (the other is "Where Shall My Wandering
Soul Begin," # 342 UMH). The questions that are posed in the

opening verses help to build the dramatic tension toward the personal statement of faith that brings this powerful poem to its conclusion.

Verse One: "Gain an interest in the Savior's blood" does not mean to become "interested" in the topic. It is "interest" more in the sense of having an "interest," or some investment or involvement, in a business. Can it be that we could gain something from the death of this God-man?

Verse Two: As he so often does, Charles Wesley puts his finger on the heart of the matter: the very idea of the Immortal dying is a mystery. Who can understand it? Not even angels' minds can comprehend it.

Verse Three: It is the definition of mercy that God would come and die for us. Immense and free indeed! "Emptied himself of all but love" is a reference to the famous hymn of Philippians 2:5-11 that speaks of Jesus emptying himself.

Verse Four: "My heart was free": the center of who we are experiences what we are made for—freedom! It is not the freedom to do anything that we want, but the freedom to "follow thee"; we act not out of a sense of coercion, but because following Christ is the best way to use our freedom.

Verse Five: No condemnation is to be dreaded now. With our sins washed away, we can boldly approach the eternal throne. No longer are we cowering like Isaiah and Peter were after their encounters with holiness, but we have been clothed in righteousness and can find our true peace in God's presence.

See also "Jesus, Lover of My Soul" (# 479 UMH) by Charles Wesley.

Suggestions for Further Reading

See Alister E. McGrath's *Christian Theology: An Introduction* (Cambridge: Blackwell Publishers, 1993, 1996) and *The Christian Theology Reader* (Cambridge: Blackwell Publishers, 1995) for an overview of some of the historic theories of the atonement. C. S. Lewis's *Mere Christianity* (New York: Macmillan, 1952) is also a helpful source of reflections on the incarnation and the atonement.

Questions for Reflection or Discussion

• If faith is "what you can rest your weight on," what is it that you have faith in? What is the problem with resting your weight on any of the following: your personal abilities; the opinion that others have of you; the prestige of your job? In what way is the community of faith something that you can rest your weight on?

• Have you ever been freely and completely forgiven by another person? What did that feel like? Envision the possibility of God forgiving all of your sinfulness. What does that feel like? Can you envision God forgetting your sin and setting it as far from you as the "east is from the west" (Psalm 103:12)? That is the good news! Could there be any better news?

• Consider the mysteries that define your life. What are they? How do those mysteries compare with the mysteries of forgiveness, joy, peace, and love that Christianity extends?

• Why is it hard to forgive other people when they wrong you? Have you considered the possibility that you do not forgive because you have not truly experienced God's forgiveness? What difference could there be in your relationships if you felt completely forgiven by God?

Notes

[1] See his "Salvation by Faith," sermon 1, 120.

[2] Review chapter 1, "John Wesley's Vision of Heart Religion—Orthokardia."

[3] Sermon 1, 120.

[4] Sermon 5, "Justification by Faith," 189. The scripture reference Wesley gives is Romans 3:25.

[5] See "Suggestions for Further Reading" at the end of the chapter.

Chapter Four

The House of Religion: The House of Holiness

We have seen that the Christian journey really begins when we have an encounter with holiness that leads us to see that we are not who we should be. This "porch" of repentance puts us in a position to accept in simple trust the forgiveness that Jesus brought into the world—to walk through the "door" of faith. We are not who we should be, but God has forgiven us! In this chapter we will try to understand the nature of the life whose center is the mystery of the forgiveness of sin, or to use Wesley's image, the house of religion that we enter by crossing over the porch of repentance and passing through the door of faith. This house is "holiness." In this chapter we want to see just how holiness is brought about in a human life and how it is connected to the "door" of faith. First, though, let us understand how Wesley understood this "holiness" that is to define our lives as believers.

Holiness As Love

In many places in his writings, John Wesley said that human beings are made for happiness and that the only way to achieve real happiness is to achieve holiness.[1] While holiness might seem a daunting or even pretentious goal for human life, Wesley saw it as what scripture required of believers.[2] So just what is this holiness that no believer shall attain heaven without? Wesley saw holiness as nothing more or less than love.[3] Let us consider several scripture passages that illustrate Wesley's belief that the biblical view of the final goal of life is a life of love.

Mark 12:28-34

(Parallels in Matthew 22:34-40 and Luke 10:25-28)
This passage contains the famous "great commandment." Jesus is confronted by a scribe who asks him, "Which commandment is the first of all?" To this Jesus answers by quoting Deuteronomy 6:4, saying, "Hear, O Israel: the Lord our God, the Lord is one; you shall love the Lord your God with all your heart, and with all your soul, and with all your mind, and with all your strength" (Mark 12: 29-30). Jesus then continues by saying, "The second is this, 'You shall love your neighbor as yourself.' There is no other commandment greater than these" (v. 31).

This last commandment can be found in Leviticus 19:18. In just a few verses of Mark, Jesus quotes two different passages from the Hebrew scriptures in order to sum up the Jewish law. Moreover, he is boldly addressing this summary to one who would be in a position to correct his views—a Jewish scribe. But the scribe does not correct him; instead the scribe says, "You are right, Teacher" (v. 32). This dual commandment to love God and love our neighbor, then, is the core of Jewish spirituality.

But it is not just an idle historical point that Jesus makes by summarizing the law in this way, for he also specifically endorses this summary. After the scribe says that such love of God and neighbor is "much more important than all whole burnt offerings and sacrifices" (v. 33), Jesus says that he has "answered wisely" and that he is "not far from the kingdom of God" (v. 34). Love is to be the basic orientation, the basic disposition, of every believer's heart.

John 13:34-35

In this short but powerful passage in John, Jesus offers the commandment to his disciples to love one another.

This is a radical and challenging passage for all who want to claim the title Christian for themselves: you will be known as a disciple of Christ's if you are a loving person. The reader might be familiar with the chorus of a simple church song "We Are One in the Spirit" that expresses this same fundamental point: "They'll know we are Christians by our love, by our love." This is an example of how sometimes the most profound statements are also the most simple: followers of Christ are people who are known for their love.

1 Corinthians 8:1-3

This passage shows the importance of love by comparing it to another highly desired virtue: knowledge. The Jews in Paul's age highly valued learning and education; to be highly educated is an admirable goal in our present age as well, for people of all religions. Paul puts knowledge in the proper perspective, however, when he says, "Knowledge puffs up, but love builds up. Anyone who claims to know something does not yet have the necessary knowledge; but anyone who loves God is known by him" (vv. 1-3). The context of this passage is Paul's discussion of whether Christians could eat food offered to idols, but the broad principle applies to our present concern: Love is to be more desired than even learning and erudition.

Why Should We Love? From the "Door" into the "House"

We have seen that love is clearly the highest virtue in the Scriptures and so characterizes the "house of religion." Let us now consider how this love is related to the "door of faith." For, as John Wesley said, faith is not the end or the highest goal of life; faith is but the door that leads into love, it is the "handmaid to love."[4] To see this connection, let us again turn to scripture.

Luke 7:36-47

In this passage, Jesus goes to a Pharisee's house for a meal. It is in this house that a woman who was "a sinner" apparently heard Jesus preaching the good news and felt her sins forgiven. She immediately felt compelled to lead a life of gratitude and love, starting with the anointing of Jesus' feet. Jesus explains this behavior by telling the parable of the two debtors (vv 41-43). Who is most loving? The one who has been forgiven the most. Why is this woman so loving? Precisely because she was such a great sinner and has been forgiven.

This is perhaps one of the clearest examples in all of scripture that the forgiveness of sins leads to a life of love, that is, the door of faith leads to the house of holiness, which is love. The end of the passage also gives us a working hypothesis we can bring to our encounters with unloving people: "The one to whom little is forgiven, loves little." When we are confronted with people who seem closed-in on themselves and are bitter, it is a good working hypothesis to assume that they do not feel forgiven, that they feel judged. Such people (indeed, all of us when we are drawn into such moods) need to be reminded of God's love for us, expressed in the death of Jesus and the forgiveness of our sins.

On that rock we can erect the kind of lasting joy that goes beyond the superficial, insipid giddiness that so often passes for joy. (It is such false displays of "joy" that often cause people to become embittered and cynical about the realities of Christianity.) At those times that we are feeling judged (and at times we will), we must, as the hymn puts it, "Turn your eyes upon Jesus." We must be reminded of the source of our life of love: God's forgiveness. For now, let us consider another scripture passage that links the "door" to the "house."

1 John 4:19-21

The First Letter of John is a tremendous source of reflections on the power of love, but I will focus on three verses in the fourth chapter:

> We love because he first loved us. Those who say, "I love God," and hate their brothers or sisters, are liars; for those who do not love a brother or sister whom they have seen, cannot love God whom they have not seen. The commandment we have from him is this: those who love God must love their brothers and sisters also.

On verse nineteen, "We love because he first loved us," Wesley wrote, "This is the sum of all religion, the genuine model of Christianity. None can say more: why should any one say less, or less intelligibly?"[5] This shows us that it is God's love reaching out to us "while we still were sinners" (Rom. 5:8) that allows us (in fact compels us as only unconditional love can compel) to live out this love toward both God and others. Why should we love? Because we have been forgiven. Because we have been forgiven we can drop the worldly pretenses of innocence and superiority that we show to our fellow humans and freely love them as our equals—sinners all, but forgiven sinners.

This link between our forgiveness and our capacity to love is seen not only in scripture but also in other Christian writing. Perhaps the greatest example of this appears in one of the classics by Victor Hugo.

Jean Valjean in *Les Misérables*

Jean Valjean is the central character in Victor Hugo's greatest novel *Les Misérables* (1862). Not only have millions of people read this story, but millions more have seen it on the stage as one of the most popular musicals of all time. Spelling out all of the twists and turns of the plot is not necessary in order for us to see that the character of Valjean shows how forgiveness of our sins can lead us to a life of love. The event that gives his life its most decisive turn illustrates what Wesley meant by moving from the door of faith into the house of holiness.

After Valjean is paroled from a nineteen-year term in prison for stealing bread to feed his sister's seven children, he is a bitter man. A bishop (whom Valjean assumes to be only a priest) takes Valjean into his house, and while the bishop and the household are asleep, Valjean steals the basket of silver from the cupboard and takes off. When the police find him with the incriminating silver, Valjean offers the preposterous story that the priest has given him the silver, that he is not stealing it at all. When they take Valjean back to the bishop's house, Valjean sees his life of freedom ending and the prospects of prison looming once again.

The bishop, instead of confirming the suspicions of the police, tells them that Valjean is right, that the silver was a gift and that it now belongs to Valjean! Not only that, but the bishop says, "I gave you the candlesticks also, which are silver like the rest, . . . Why did you not take them along with your plates?" The bishop speaks solemnly to the forgiven thief, "Jean Valjean, my brother: you belong no longer to evil, but to good. It is your soul that I am buying for you. . . . and I give it to God!"

At that moment of receiving not only forgiveness but also the means to achieve wealth, Valjean vows that this totally unmerited gift will lead to a new quality of life. The story continues by showing how Valjean opens a factory that gives people jobs, how he cares for one of his workers even to the extent of taking personal responsibility for her fatherless child after the woman dies. He goes on to selflessly aid this adopted daughter's fiancé when the young man's life is in danger. Most dramatically, Valjean saves the life of the very policeman who has chased Valjean over the years.

Time and again Valjean shows the profound Christian love that comes from being set free from the old life of sin and being made free for a life of love. Forgiveness, when fully understood, leads to a life of holiness. But having seen these connections between forgiveness and love, it is now time to be more specific about just what is meant by Christian love.

What Is "Love"?

Many of the most basic concepts in Christianity are also some of the most misunderstood. No concept is more misunderstood, however, than love, because we so often use the word in a way that avoids its most important Christian meaning.

On television or in movies, when someone says to somebody else, "I just want to love you," we know what is in store for us. Immediately the slow saxophone music will rise in the background, the protagonists will start to kiss, and clothes will start coming off. In our popular culture, love equals sex. We can see this connection most clearly when people try to justify their premarital or extramarital sexual liaisons by saying, "What is wrong with loving another person?" It sounds as if they are giving a high-minded and even Christian defense of their actions, when in fact they have not grasped what Christian love is all about. As we have done previously, let us go to the scriptures for our definition of this key term.

1 John 3:10-24

One key verse that gives us a concise definition of love is verse 16: "We know love by this, that he laid down his life for us—and we ought to lay down our lives for one another." Jesus' death on the cross is not only the means for the forgiveness of our sins, it is the ultimate example of love.

Love defined by the total self-giving of Jesus on the cross is radically different from love-as-sex. In fact, the Greek language in which the New Testament was originally written has several different words for love. *Eros* is the word used to describe erotic love in Greek, while *agape* is the self-giving love of God. It is unfortunate that English translates these two quite different realities with the same word, but theologians have written much about the importance of maintaining the original distinctions.[6] While this distinctively Christian notion of love as defined by Jesus on the cross is helpful in distinguishing Christian love from pleasure-seeking sexuality, it might seem to be too dramatic an example to be useful in an everyday way for many people. For a fuller elaboration of this love depicted by the cross of Christ, and a description of it that puts it in everyday terms that we can apply to our lives, we turn to one of the most famous passages in the Bible.

1 Corinthians 13

People choose to have this passage read at their weddings more than any other passage in the Bible, and with good reason. In this beautiful chapter Paul describes the nature of true agape love. While the whole chapter is definitely worth reading, I reproduce here a whole lifetime's agenda compressed into just over four verses:

> Love is patient; love is kind; love is not envious or boastful or arrogant or rude. It does not insist on its own way; it is not irritable or resentful; it does not rejoice in wrongdoing, but rejoices in the truth. It bears all things, believes all things, hopes all things, endures all things. Love never ends (vv. 4-8).

When we read these words, we see just how far Christian love is from sexual desire. Of course, Christianity is not somehow anti-sexual—far from it! But love is more than the warm feelings you have when you are alone with your special person. In fact, this definition of love should remind us that the religious affections, as Wesley described them, are not the same as feelings. According to these definitions from scripture, we can see that love is not merely a feeling. It is positive energy spent in a relationship, it is living for the well-being of others, being patient with others and not resentful, bearing all things, having a caring orientation to others that does not end. Feelings come and go, but this love "never ends."

This one feature of agape, above all others, should make clear that it comes from God alone and is beyond our measly human capacities. No one can "pull themselves up by their bootstraps" into a love that "never ends." This love grows when we direct our attention to the object that can generate it: Jesus on the cross, dying for us before we even knew him, let alone loved him.[7]

This love can take many forms and can be expressed in such a wide variety of ways that I will not try to catalog them. But one passage of scripture helps to show the kind of company that this love keeps, the kind of virtues that surround it and grow from it. This passage appears in another of Paul's letters.

Galatians 5:22-24: The Fruit of the Spirit

In Galatians 5, after describing some of the ways of life that the Christian should avoid (the "works of the flesh"), Paul describes character traits that the Christian should seek after and nurture in his or her own soul with the help of the Holy Spirit. These he terms the "fruit of the Spirit." This list of nine virtues was one of John Wesley's favorite summaries of holiness. The fruit that grows when the Holy Spirit is in our lives consists of "love, joy, peace, patience, kindness, generosity, faithfulness, gentleness, and self-control" (vv. 22-23). Wesley, in commenting on this passage, said that "love is the Root of all the rest,"[8] meaning that once true love has taken root in one's heart, the rest of these virtues will start to grow as well. One can in fact notice a number of parallels between this passage and Paul's definition of love in 1 Corinthians, where love itself is seen as patient and kind.

So whether it is expressed as these nine portions of the "fruit of the Spirit" or more compactly expressed simply as "love," the goal or end of the Christian life, the true house of religion, is a character that is defined by—and lives out of—this orientation of patience, joyousness, kindness, and generosity. If all of our behavior can be traced back to this motivation of love, then we have arrived at what Wesley called *sanctification* or *perfection*. Since those terms can cause people some trouble, let us spend a moment reflecting on what Wesley meant and did not mean by them.

Sanctification and Perfection

Wesley saw many people living out the Christian life as if it consisted almost entirely of the porch and door of religion—that is, they made faith the end of the journey. In the groups of people that started gathering around him, Wesley began challenging them with what he took to be a scriptural question. Even today, when people are ordained in The United Methodist Church they are asked this same question: "Are you going on to perfection?"

On hearing this question, some might invoke the "porch" of religion and claim that the humility that should flow from our repentance should prevent us from ever making such a claim. This, however, would be a misunderstanding of Wesley's views. The question is not "Are you perfect?" but is instead "Are you *going on* to perfection?" To say no to that question would be, for Wesley, a violation of the Lord's own commandments. Let us turn to scripture to see in what way this talk of perfection could be justified and how we can understand it.

Matthew 5:43-48: Being Perfect in Love

In the middle of the "Sermon on the Mount" (chapters 5–7 of Matthew), Jesus says this:

> You have heard that it was said, "You shall love your neighbor and hate your enemy." But I say to you, Love your enemies and pray for those who persecute you, so that you may be children of your Father in heaven; for he makes his sun rise on the evil and on the good, and sends rain on the righteous and the unrighteous. For if you love those who love you, what reward do you have? Do not even the tax collectors do the same? And if you greet only your brothers and sisters, what more are you doing than others? Do not even the Gentiles do the same? Be perfect, therefore, as your heavenly Father is perfect.

If one takes the last verse of the passage out of context, it might seem like a call to endless anxiety. Who can be mistake-free? Who can have perfect knowledge? Who can have perfect social skills or physical abilities? Who could take such a passage seriously without going crazy? The key to understanding this verse about perfection, however, comes (as it so often does when interpreting scripture) when we see the context of the remark.

This whole passage is about loving not only the people whom it is easy or even "natural" to love, but also loving our enemies. If we grow in the Christian life so much that the disposition to love is fixed firmly in our hearts, if our eyes focus so consistently on the object of our faith—Jesus Christ—that we can do nothing but love all whom we encounter, whether or not they are "friendly" or "lovable," then we are "going on to perfection." In his many writings explaining Jesus' call to perfection as a call to perfect love, Wesley tried to deal with many of the objections to perfection.[9] While I need not rehearse here all of the misunderstandings and polemics that surrounded this issue in Wesley's time, it is crucial for our purposes to see that perfection for Wesley meant nothing more or less than the scriptural injunction to love all, including our enemies.

When "Perfection" Does Not Feel Perfect

Wesley defined a sinful act as "the voluntary transgression of a known law of God."[10] Since Wesley saw love as the summary of the law and the goal of all Christian living, anything consciously done against love could be seen as a sin. (The works of the flesh in Galatians 5:16-21 are examples.) A problem arises, however, when people move closer and closer to the goal of perfect love in all of their actions, and do feel themselves dying to sin and being forgiven by God, yet they feel depressed or alienated, separated from God or spiritually dry. There can be many reasons for this.

Sometimes spiritual dryness comes because we have confused the religious affections with feelings. We need to remember at these times that God is not expecting us to have a constant stream of "good feelings" when God calls us to a life of perfect love. While the "peace that passes understanding" is to be ours, we will not be conscious of it at all times. But this should not cripple our spiritual lives; we need not *feel* loving to do a loving act. Remember the discussion in the first chapter where we established that the affections or emotions of the spiritual life that are genuine are the ones that lead us to behave with holiness in the world, not ones that somehow lead to uninterrupted bliss.

Even once we understand that our feelings will come and go, it can also be helpful to understand some of the more common reasons for this. Sometimes it can be attributed to an incomplete repentance—not confessing some sin or not turning to God completely. Wesley and many other spiritual writers often spoke of a "darling sin" or a "bosom sin" or a "secret sin"—the one behavior, thought, disposition, relationship, that we will not yield to the discipline of God's holy love. To ignore this possibility when examining our spiritual lives is to ignore how deeply rooted sin can be in our nature. As we grow in our walk with God, we will uncover new areas of sinfulness, and we will continue to walk over that porch of repentance and through the door of faith.

Sometimes, however, spiritual dryness can come not from actual sinfulness but from our being bombarded by temptations. Wesley was very clear that temptations will not cease this side of heaven.[11] While we ought not to seek them out, we should not be surprised when they seek us out. While we would hope that all of our life is spent in doing good works out of a spirit of love, in reality there are times when the best we can do is avoid sin. That is why Wesley wrote and published a sermon titled "Heaviness through Manifold Temptations."[12] *Heaviness* was a term used in the eighteenth century for what we would call depression; Wesley knew that fighting off temptations can sometimes leave us little energy for other things. We should not feel guilty about that, but simply let God's spirit carry us through the trying time and remember that, like Paul "whenever I am weak, then I am strong" (2 Cor. 12:10).

Spiritual dryness—our failure to experience the "fruit of the Spirit"—can come from yet another cause, however. Our heart-life can be impoverished if we ignore the fact that Jesus came into the world not only to teach and to forgive sin, but also to heal. Needing healing is not the same as needing forgiveness.[13]

In one of his sermons explaining what he meant by "perfection," Wesley said that being perfect in love will not lead us to perfection in knowledge. Therefore, we can make mistakes and fall into inadvertent sins (which Wesley would not call sins, strictly speaking since they are not deliberate violations of a known law of God). For example, someone who acts only from the motivation of love still might do something that could be interpreted by someone else as unloving. If I take a blind person's arm and help him across the street, I might have been acting out of love, but unless he asked for help, my actions might be offensive to him. He might interpret my behavior as an act of condescension or a slight of his abilities to function in the world. Since we are not made perfect in our knowledge of people and their histories, even those acting on love will make mistakes. See Wesley's sermon on perfection (# 40) and his *Plain Account of Christian Perfection*; the latter contains some important footnotes on understanding particular features of perfection. In this same sermon, Wesley also says that being perfect in love will not free us from what he called our "infirmities." We can expand this understanding of "infirmities" in ways that will help us understand the ups and downs of the spiritual life.

When looking at their individual past histories, some people think that they need constantly to put their finger in their open psychic wounds, or even reopen old wounds. This behavior is close to what I spoke about earlier as "regret" and "remorse." When we do this, we need to recognize that these are self-delusional half-measures, and what is needed instead is true repentance.[14] But there is another necessary dimension for dealing with this kind of psychic "infirmity": an awareness of God's desire to heal those old wounds so that they never need bother us again.

I understand that talk about "healing" can be off-putting and even scary. Many people have been turned off to Christianity by showy "healing" ministries that act as if being in the right relationship with God will take away all obstacles we encounter in our embodied existence. While I do not deny that physical healings do take place, it seems true that God does not always choose to work in that way. In 2 Corinthians 12:7-10

Paul says that he prayed three times to be delivered from his "thorn in the flesh," but God did not take it away. In this, Paul found that "whenever I am weak, then I am strong" (v. 10), another testimony that when we name in repentance and confession not only our failings but also our inabilities, we have access to true power, the power of God. Besides, the mortality rate of all Christians is 100 percent—there is no escaping the fact that we all must pass through death. So I am talking about something other than—and even more important than—physical healing.

Our human life entails many painful episodes. If anyone does not think that normal growth entails pain then they have never been around a teething baby! More to our point than this example of physical pain, psychic pains are involved in such normal and expected life changes as adolescence, the adjustments of marriage, or losing loved ones to death. In some lives, the pain and woundedness—the infirmities—take even more pointed and dramatic forms, such as divorce, incest, rape, and other such traumas.

The spiritual question is not "How can I avoid all pain?" since no one can. The point instead is to acknowledge our real pain and brokenness as a part of true repentance. If repentance is "true self-knowledge" then we need not only to confess our sinfulness but also to proclaim our "infirmities"—our brokenness, our pain and suffering, and our need for healing. The question then becomes: What do I do with the pain and brokenness that I have experienced? The answer is this: Our infirmities and brokenness do not need forgiveness; they did not result from my deliberate violation of a known law of God. What they need instead is healing.

Many people have spoken at various retreats I have attended about the thrilling discovery of God's healing power in their spiritual lives. Whether our brokenness stems from the trauma of sexual abuse, or deep grief over the death of a loved one, or the psychic scarring of the horrors of war (or even seemingly "smaller"—but nonetheless potent—experiences such as memories of grade-school humiliation), we all need to put the past behind us and be healed from the particularities of our own growing process. Not, of course, to forget them but to be freed from the power they have over us. This need can, of course, be addressed by secular counselors, and I would not wish to deny the helpful role that they can play. But, as Christians, we finally need to ask God for this kind of deep healing, so that we can go into the future with all of our energy freed. We then can live a life marked by the fruit of the Holy Spirit. The God who saved us also wants to heal us so that we can fully enjoy God's blessings.[15]

Wesley may not have included healing in his summary of the three great doctrines of Christianity—repentance, faith, and holy love—but in his practice as a spiritual guide and friend he knew that healing was an integral part of the Christian's growth into wholeness.

A Neglected Expression of Love: Friendship

When we see the Christian life defined as a life of love, and when we see this love further defined by Christ's giving of himself on the cross (1 John 3:16), we might come to believe that the only way to be a good Christian is to die a heroic death for the sake of another. Going from a worldly orientation of self-love to the radical servant love of others to which Jesus calls us might seem an impossible leap. Without for a moment denying the goal of humble servanthood, we should realize that there are realistic and achievable steps that we can take in order to move from the self-love of pride to the servant love of Christ.

First of all, we need to see that people do not have to "give their lives" in the literal kind of way that Jesus did in order to follow his commands. The quote from 1 Corinthians 13 makes this clear. A good mother, for instance, often lays down her life for her children not all at once in some dramatic way, but in numerous small ways over the course of many years, through countless acts that reflect patience, kindness, and steadfastness. "Giving one's life" can and should be a project that stretches out for as many days, weeks, or years as we have life.

But in taking this project as our own, we need to find role models for our behavior other than the selfless mother. Without denying the importance of good mothers and fathers (and while decrying the all-too-frequent lack of the same in our world today), we must remember that Jesus said even the unbelievers are capable of showing this kind of love of kin (Matt. 5:46). We as Christians are called to love not just our children, but even our enemies, with a servant love. As a way to approach the goal of self-giving agape love, we need to look to something that is readily accessible to all, regardless of our family relationships. We also need not start with the most dramatic example as our immediate goal. As babies in Christ, to use Paul's metaphor, we need to start with milk and not with meat (1 Cor. 3:1, 2). An orientation toward others that can start us on the path to full agape, something that takes us out of ourselves and beyond our family bonds (without denying them), is friendship.

This kind of friendship does not mean being involved in "affinity groups" where everyone is like us and is interested in the same things that interest us. Instead, this friendship entails reaching out across our normal boundaries. Once we are in the habit of relating to other people as friends, we can begin to start relating to even our enemies as friends. The best way to do away with an enemy is to make him a friend. This is the most exciting, challenging, and, finally, the most rewarding thing that we can do in this life. I do not think that it is a coincidence that in one of the world's most popular movies—*It's a Wonderful Life*—the key line in the last scene is "No man is a failure who has friends."

"But, wait a minute!" you might say. "Being a friend means trusting and sharing, and enemies will just use that trust to take advantage of us." This is true. We must acknowledge that a delicate dance takes place between, on the one hand, our character (marked by the traits or virtues that we call the "fruit of the Spirit"), and on the other hand, the world that we relate to outside of ourselves. We must remember that when Jesus said "Love your enemies," he was not saying "Act as if no one is your enemy." There are people and forces in the world that hate the good news, people who would rather live in prideful self-deception about who they are and who God is. No Christian is asked to deny that we live in a world populated with many such people.

What we are called to do in growing toward an agape form of love is to recognize the real differences between all of the different people in the world. (In this context, some people speak of recognizing true "otherness.") Not everyone is leading (or is even trying to lead, or even wants to lead) a life of agape love. Some even take on the role as the "enemy" or perverter or would-be manipulator of those who lead a life of servant love. Only when we recognize these truths will we be following Jesus' directive to be "as wise as serpents" even as we are being as "innocent as doves" (Matt. 10:16). Only when we have such a clear-eyed view of the world will we have "counted the cost" of entering into the battle with sin and death so that we can commit to the conflict both realistically and unreservedly. Discerning the "signs of the times" was the task of the biblical prophets; so must it be the task of all who want to live out the call to love. Only when it is directed by the humble and fallible—yet necessary—acts of spiritual discernment can our love be effective in the world.

Such a life of loving service, shaped and directed by the discernment of the Holy Spirit, is a life that meets our very human, very deep, desire for adventure, challenge, and drama!

That is an agenda worthy of people created for freedom, a freedom best fulfilled in obedience, no matter what persecution and rejection the world has in store for us. The life of loving our enemies is the true path to happiness.

You will remember that Wesley said that we are made for happiness, and that happiness comes only from achieving holiness. We can now expand on that statement by saying that since holiness is love—especially love of our enemies—then happiness is best understood as a by-product of loving service. This leads us to one final deduction:

Happiness is an evaluation, not a feeling.

If happiness comes from holiness, and holiness is all about leading a life of self-giving love (which in turn comes from knowing that our sins are forgiven), then we need not worry about seeking out the feeling of happiness. In fact, if we focus our attention on our feelings, we will lose sight not only of God—the source of our forgiveness and love—but also of the neighbor we are called to love. Happiness is our evaluation that we are leading the kind of life that we were made for, namely, the completely fulfilling life of holiness. It will come as a by-product of our paying attention to what we are called to pay attention to: God and our neighbor. This, I think, is the most profound meaning of Jesus' statement that "Those who find their life will lose it, and those who lose their life for my sake will find it" (Matt. 10:39).

We should understand happiness as the deepest sense that we are on the right course, that we are living out a life of being who we are called to be. But this is also how we should understand those other key words in the Christian vocabulary: *peace* and *joy*. At the deepest level, happiness, holiness, joy, and peace are all the same as holy agape love. That is why Wesley termed it the "house itself." It is where we are called to live.

In the next chapter, I turn to the question of how to grow and foster Wesley's vision for heart religion today. How are repentance, faith, and love grown and expressed in contemporary life? What would Christian life aimed at this goal of heart religion look like today? Just how are we to fix our attention on God and our neighbor so that we might love them, and what specifically does this call to love entail?

Pertinent Sermons of John Wesley

"The Circumcision of the Heart" (sermon 17); "The Marks of the New Birth" (sermon 18); "The Great Privilege of Those That Are Born of God" (sermon 19).

Wesleyan Hymn on Love

"Love Divine, All Loves Excelling"
(#384 UMH)

> Love divine, all loves excelling,
> joy of heaven, to earth come down;
> fix in us thy humble dwelling;
> all thy faithful mercies crown!
> Jesus, thou art all compassion,
> pure, unbounded love thou art;
> visit us with thy salvation;
> enter every trembling heart.
>
> Breathe, O breathe thy loving Spirit
> into every troubled breast!
> Let us all in thee inherit,
> let us find that second rest.
> Take away our bent to sinning;
> Alpha and Omega be;
> end of faith, as its beginning,
> set our hearts at liberty.
>
> Come, Almighty to deliver,
> let us all thy life receive;

suddenly return and never,
nevermore thy temples leave.
Thee we would be always blessing,
serve thee as thy hosts above,
pray and praise thee without ceasing,
glory in thy perfect love.

Finish, then, thy new creation;
pure and spotless let us be.
Let us see thy great salvation
perfectly restored in thee;
changed from glory into glory,
till in heaven we take our place,
till we cast our crowns before thee,
lost in wonder, love, and praise.

Notes on "Love Divine, All Loves Excelling"

This hymn, written in 1747, is one of the most widely sung of Charles Wesley's hymns. In the hymnal of 1780 it was placed in the section titled "For Believers Groaning for Full Redemption," which justly captures the essence of the call to perfection.

Verse One: The agape love of God is the love that truly "excels" all other loves. It is this love that we want to come to earth, to be embodied, to find a home in our humble dwelling, our human hearts.

Verse Two: It is the Holy Spirit that brings this love to us. The Holy Spirit draws us down the path toward perfect love, by lessening our sinful and selfish desires. This is what is meant by taking away our "bent" to sinning. Alpha and Omega are the beginning and the end of the Greek alphabet, just as God's holiness is both the beginning and the end of our Christian life.

Verse Three: When Charles Wesley asks "let us all thy life receive," he knows that this will lead to a life that is marked by continuous blessings from God. This means not wealth and fame but the joyous chance to serve God, as the many in heaven do.

Verse Four: The process of sanctification—becoming holy—prepares us not only for a life of deeper and deeper love, but it prepares us for heaven. When we take our place there, we will cast our crowns—the symbols of our self-centered, prideful existence—gladly before God's throne. What will heaven be like? Wesley gives us a foretaste by saying that it will be marked by "wonder, love, and praise." Seeing "wonder" in heaven is a good reminder of the mystery that is a part of life. Mystery is not always something to be worried over; it also can be celebrated, as in "wonder."

See also # 566 (UMH), "Blest Be the Dear Uniting Love," or # 422 (UMH), "Jesus, Thine All-Victorious Love," both by Charles Wesley.

Suggestions for Further Reading

Wesley's fullest explanation of "perfection" was in *A Plain Account of Christian Perfection* (London: The Epworth Press, 1952). See *Five Views on Sanctification* (Grand Rapids, MI: Zondervan Publishing House, 1987) for five different denominational views on this topic. For a beautiful analysis of the four different conceptions of love in the Greek language see C. S. Lewis's *The Four Loves* (Harcourt, Brace & Company, 1991).

Questions for Reflection or Discussion

• What honestly comes to your mind when you hear the word love? Are they images that come from our sex-oriented culture, or do they come from the gospel?

• If you think that someone "loves" you, what criteria do you use to decide? Do worldly things such as sexual desirability, popularity, or wealth make for love?

- Without looking at 1 Corinthians 13, would you be able to give a definition of love?

- Do you find yourself being impatient very often in your day? If so, do you realize that just so far as you are impatient to that same extent you are unloving (1 Corinthians 13:4)? Try to recall specific instances of your own impatience, and imagine how you might react differently, knowing that your self-identity as a loving person depends on your being patient. If impatience is not your particular sin, you might ask the same questions of yourself regarding unkindness, envy, boastfulness, arrogance, rudeness, irritability, or resentment.

- Have you thought seriously about what it would mean to embody a love that "never ends"? If you find the thought scary or intimidating, it could be that you have forgotten that such love comes from God. It is not a love that is defined by feelings, but by serving. Can you name someone in your own experience who embodies this love? What behavioral evidence can you offer for your judgment that someone is living a life of agape?

Notes

[1] See Wesley's comments on John 12:36, Hebrews 2:3, and Hebrews 12:11 in his *Explanatory Notes Upon the New Testament*. See also Outler's introduction to the *Sermons*, vol. I, 35; note 28, sermon 6, "The Righteousness of Faith," 213; and sermon 7, "The Way to the Kingdom," 223.

[2] See, for example, 2 Corinthians 7:1; Hebrews 12:14; 1 Peter 1:15-16; 1 John 3:2-3.

[3] See Outler's note to page 223 of Wesley's *Sermons*, vol. I, for references to holiness-as-love in Wesley's sermons.

[4] A handmaid in the medieval sense is one who helped a more "important" person by performing certain necessary functions for that person. In this metaphorical sense of the term as Wesley is using it, philosophy was often called the "handmaid"

to theology: it helped the theologian in certain ways but was not an end in itself. Faith is specifically called the handmaid to love in Wesley's sermon 36, "The Law Established through Faith, vol. II," 38.

[5] *Explanatory Notes Upon the New Testament*, comment on 1 John 4:19 (London: Charles H. Kelly), 915.

[6] See C. S. Lewis's *The Four Loves* (San Diego: Harcourt, Brace & Company, 1971) for an accessible treatment of this issue.

[7] If you want to explore the theological issues that surround this question of how God's love becomes our love, see my article "John Wesley's Heart Religion and the Righteousness of Christ" in Methodist History, vol. XXXV, No. 3, April 1997, 148–156.

[8] *Explanatory Notes Upon the New Testament*, 697.

[9] See sermon 40, "Christian Perfection."

[10] See sermon 8, "The First-Fruits of the Spirit," 240, and Outler's note #52; sermon 19, "The Great Privilege of those that are Born of God," 436.

[11] See "Christian Perfection," sermon 40, especially the whole first section where Wesley explains that perfection does not mean freedom from imperfect knowledge, ignorance, infirmities, or temptations.

[12] Sermon 47.

[13] See here the works of Flora Slosson Wuellner, especially *Prayer, Stress, and Our Inner Wounds* (Nashville, TN: The Upper Room, 1985) and *Release: Healing from Wounds of Family, Church, and Community* (Nashville, TN: Upper Room Books, 1996).

[14] Review chapter 2.

[15] Forgiveness and healing are often intertwined in the process of growing in maturity as a Christian, as Wesley himself knew. Much has been written about this connection. See the works of Flora Slosson Wuellner and David Seamands.

Chapter Five

Living a Heart Religion in the World Today: The Fears and Hopes of Heart Religion Revisited

 We have seen how the Christian spiritual journey becomes energized when we are confronted by holiness, and that this holiness leads us to repentance, to a trust that our sins are forgiven, and to a growth toward holiness ourselves. The journey that starts with holiness ends with holiness. In this final chapter, I want to provide answers to the simple question "How?" How are we to attain this heart religion today? How are we able to encounter the holiness that leads us to repentance? How are we to grow in the faith that Jesus' death brought about our forgiveness? How are we to grow in the love that makes us holy? In answering these questions I also will address the hopes and concerns about heart religion first raised in chapter 1 and show how Wesley's "house of religion" metaphor of Christian spirituality fulfills the hopes and avoids the pitfalls mentioned there. I will begin this task by first pointing out the greatest drawback of this image of the "house of religion."

What the "House" Image Leaves Out: The Continual Nature of Formation

While Wesley's compact doctrinal summary has many benefits, it does invite one important misunderstanding—namely, that one need take only one trip across the "porch" and through the "door" in order to be once and for all "in the house." For Wesley, as well as for the rest of the mainstream of Christian orthodoxy, repentance and trust in Christ are to be daily features of the Christian life, not just vague memories of a summer camp conversion experience, an altar call, a baptism, or a confirmation ritual of many years ago. Subsequent experiences may not be as dramatic as our first one, but they are also important. The house of religion is something that we need to enter into consciously each day of our lives.

While there is nothing wrong with remembering past spiritual highlights of our lives—and in fact there are many good things about occasionally rehearsing such holy memories—God wants to meet us not only in our remembrance of things past, but also in the living vitality of the present. Perhaps we can put this "house of religion" image into the context of ongoing formation if we see it in the light of John 14:2: "In my Father's house there are many dwelling places." Each day we can cross the porch of a different mansion in our Father's house; we can walk through a new door of faith and find a whole new house of holiness, marked by a different quality of God's love.

But now we might ask: How can we experience that presence of God and grow in repentance, trust, and love in an ongoing way? In response to this, Wesley gives us three general rules to follow. His "General Rules" are basic guidelines for how to be a good disciple of Christ; he formulated them to help people in the "societies" that would become the Methodist church. In them, Wesley listed three broad categories of actions, three ways to spend the energy that God has given us.[1] These might seem like "common sense," but the problem is that they are not commonly practiced. In their simplest form, these rules are as follows: do no harm and avoid evil, do good of every possible sort to all people, and attend to all of the "ordinances of God" (what he termed the *works of piety*, or the actions that help us grow a right heart). In order to understand this lifelong agenda for spiritual formation, let us first understand the "works of piety." Then we will look at how to live out the injunctions to "do no harm" and to "do good of every possible sort" by attending to what Wesley called *works of mercy* (the actions that express our love of God and neighbor).

We must always remember in discussing these "works" that underlying them, and preceding them, is God's grace. God's loving grace goes before us and makes possible our growth, and we, in our freedom, can choose either to make use of that grace or say no to it. When we lead a life defined by following these three rules, we are responding to God's gracious initiative with a grateful "yes."

The Works of Piety or Means of Grace: Focusing Our Hearts on the Right Objects

The phrase *works of piety* may have an antiquated sound to our ears. Because of this, we need to see that what Wesley called the *works of piety*, he also called the *means of grace*. Since this latter phrase has a wider usage in Christian circles, let me use it instead in the discussions that follow.

We often use the distinction between means and ends in our everyday discourse. If someone wants to achieve a certain goal (or end), he or she has to use the appropriate tools (or means). This is the same use of *means* that Wesley had in mind. In order to achieve the goal of holiness—living completely out of a motivation to love—one has to use the means that will bring about that goal. These means are the means of grace; for Wesley they included several actions and duties that are familiar to Christians today, but also several that seem foreign or strange. Let us briefly consider these.[2]

Baptism

When considering how to grow in holiness, many might think first of baptism. But baptism is a religious action that Wesley seldom addressed, for the simple reason that virtually everyone in the England of Wesley's time was baptized in their infancy as a matter of course. Wesley did believe that baptism was the way to begin the Christian walk; that has been a basic teaching since the very beginning of the Christian church. In his work among the people, though, most everyone he encountered had already been baptized. Accordingly, Wesley assumed the reality of baptism rather than emphasized it.

It should be said, however, that the act of remembering our baptism—remembering the fact that we are baptized—can be a way to make this past action relevant to our present spiritual lives (and there are now some helpful liturgies for doing this).[3] What makes baptism unique among the "works of piety" is that it is meant to be an unrepeatable event. The other five "instituted means of grace" are all meant to be regular, ongoing practices in the Christian life. (Basically, instituted means of grace are those channels for God's grace that were ordained by God. This does not mean that God acts only through these means, but that these are the ordinary ways that God makes God's grace available to us.)[4]

Prayer

The most basic "work" of the Christian life, the most fundamental way that we should spend our energy in order to grow in grace, is prayer. Since the purpose of the works of piety is to turn our focus to God so that we might repent, have faith, and grow in love, there could be no more helpful action than to address God—and listen for God—in prayer. For Wesley, this included public prayer and family prayer as well as private prayer.

Certainly, spontaneous prayer is to be encouraged, but using prayers written by others can also be helpful in that they help us to focus our attention not on a God of our own design, but on the one true God that was known by those fathers and mothers of the faith who have gone before us. Wesley had his *Book of Common Prayer* of the Church of England to draw on; he published an abridgment of this, as well as other collections of prayers in his own lifetime.[5] One could also consult many of the books of prayers that are being published today, and most hymnals also have prayers that one can use for this purpose. Additionally, there are many excellent books that can help people get started on their prayer lives.[6]

"Searching" the Scriptures

Wesley did not want to promote the kind of Bible study that people so often engage in today, namely, a kind of dry learning of facts about one or another of the various books of the Bible. That is why he did not say "study" the Bible as a way to grow spiritually; he said "search the scriptures." The attitude implied in this latter phrase makes all the difference.

When you are searching for something, you have a specific need and you are trying to satisfy that need. For example, when you are searching for your keys, you have a very clear objective and a clear motivation. Similarly, when you are searching for God and God's word in the Bible, you are looking with a specific awareness of your need for spiritual growth. God is more often found by those committed to the search rather than the merely curious. If we study the Bible just to pile up names, dates, and places, as if we were studying it in order to win at "Bible Trivia," the chances are great that we will miss the point entirely.

Because the Bible is the church's book, we need to do our searching in the company of other seekers and searchers within the community of faith. Ideally, this will occur under the tutelage of ones who have experience in the quest for God in the Bible. We should have no reason to try to go it alone.[7]

The Lord's Supper

In many Protestant churches in the United States today, the sacrament of the Lord's Supper (or "Holy Communion" or the Eucharist) is not celebrated frequently. This state of affairs would puzzle Wesley. In fact, Wesley himself sometimes took communion several times in the course of one week. One of the reasons that communion was not celebrated often in the early days of America was that ordained ministers were in short supply on the frontier. People had to wait for the traveling "preachers" to come to their town in order to take communion, and sometimes months would pass between visits. Too often these patterns of infrequent communion became well-entrenched habits in American churches with no underlying theological justification.

In order to see how this sacrament can direct our hearts to God, consider the words that are recited in most worship services when communion is celebrated. They are usually a quote of, or a variation on, 1 Corinthians 11:23-26, in which Paul is telling the Corinthians how to celebrate this ritual correctly:

> For I have received from the Lord what I also handed on to you, that the Lord Jesus on the night when he was betrayed took a loaf of bread, and when he had given thanks, he broke it and said, "This is my body that is for you. Do this in remembrance of me." In the same way he took the cup also, after supper, saying, "This cup is the new covenant in my blood. Do this, as often as you drink it, in remembrance of me." For as often as you eat this bread and drink the cup, you proclaim the Lord's death until he comes.

The action of remembering Christ on the cross, and then voluntarily associating ourselves with that sacrificial action by taking the bread and wine—the "body and blood" of Christ—cannot but help to orient us to God's saving act in Christ. What we need to understand is that, like the mystery of Christ on the cross, the sacrament of communion does not have to be fully understood in order to be effective. We need not become a proponent for one or another theory about how communion works; our job is to take it in faith and be formed by it.[8]

Fasting

In our culture, fasting might seem like something to do primarily in order to lose weight. Fasting for spiritual purposes might strike some as rather medieval, but Wesley knew that fasting works. How can fasting orient us to God? Many answers would shed light on fasting, but let us settle for one that goes right to the heart of the matter: When we fast, we learn to say no to ourselves; if we cannot do that, we will not get far in the spiritual life.

Fasting is the decision to abstain from an otherwise normal function for spiritual purposes.[9] When Christians fast, for example, from food, or sex, or television, they are not saying that these things are bad in themselves. Rather, they are learning to discipline themselves so that nothing masters them except God. If we cannot put our passions on hold and say no to ourselves, we cannot be free to say yes to God with all of our hearts.

While people with medical conditions need to be careful about fasting from food for extended periods of time, most people can skip a meal as a way of acknowledging our neediness and our dependence on God for what is truly filling. Wesley fasted breakfast and lunch on most Fridays (in honor of the saving events of Good Friday). Even today, all United Methodist ministers affirm at their ordination that they will recommend and practice Christian fasting. The failure to pursue this work of piety is perhaps one of the causes of the lack of focus in some of our churches today.

Christian Conference

This means of grace might seem strange to today's ears, but it was of undoubted importance to Wesley. What he meant by this term is simply getting together with other Christians regularly in order to encourage one another and, even more important, to hold each other accountable for the commitments that the Christian life calls for. These were not simply prayer or support groups. They were small groups of people who would open their hearts to each other, confess their sins and shortcomings to each other, and in that context of openness and honesty, "speak the truth in love" (Eph. 4:15) to one another.

It is easy to get caught up in self-deception when you are not receiving feedback from someone you trust. You might, for example, think of yourself as someone who is generous and a good steward of God's gifts—until you are face-to-face with someone who knows how much you actually give to church and charities! Likewise, it is easy to say in general, "I am doing the best I can as a Christian," but it involves a different level of humility, honesty, and commitment when you leave the generalities behind and allow people to ask you specific questions about your Christian "walk." These questions might include those such as "John, we know you have had a problem with gambling away your family's grocery money, so tell us: How much did you spend on lottery tickets this last week?"

In these small groups our repentance is made more permanent in very real and concrete ways. Our faithfulness and love are also quickly demonstrated when we talk about what really has been going on in our lives. Mutual trust, humility, and a loving sense of being accountable to all of the members of the group are obviously important in this kind of endeavor, so it is not something to be taken up lightly. There are, happily, some signs that this means of grace is becoming more and more widely practiced today. While several programs and books are available that describe in great detail how to make this kind of covenant group a reality,[10] the crucial ingredient is a group of people committed to God, each other, and the process of Christian growth. Wesley knew that when these elements were present, God's Holy Spirit would use them for the cause of sanctification.

The "House of Religion" As Formed by the Sunday Morning Worship Service

To varying degrees, each of these works of piety can find a home in the weekly gathered worship of local churches; when they do, the house of religion can be formed in the lives of the worshipers. Hymns and anthems can invite us to the porch of repentance by providing a sense of God's holiness. This repentance can be expressed through prayers of confession, either in silence or spoken in unison with others.

Reciting creeds and hearing the Bible preached can focus our attention on the saving act of Christ, so that we can once again consciously trust that our sins are forgiven and walk through the "door of faith." Intimate acts of trust that take place in the sanctuary, such as baptisms and funerals, can help us fully to engage the depths of our hearts with the reality of God's forgiving and comforting love.

Being a part of rituals of love and commitment—such as marriages—can deepen our disposition to love others, whether we are being married ourselves or merely celebrating the marriage of others. Prophetic preaching can show us how we should be expressing our love in the world today and how we can best fulfill our call to live in the "house of religion itself," which is love. Hymns and songs of gratitude can express our deepest sense of thanksgiving for all that we have been given.

In some Protestant communities, communion has been associated with the porch or the door only; it is often practiced only at a time of repentance and sorrow. The truth, however, is that we do not understand fully what communion has to offer us until we see that it is to be celebrated not just in times of repentance, but also in times of great joy and thanksgiving. The Eucharist should be practiced year-round, and we should allow it to take on different shades of meaning as the seasons of the church, and the seasons of our lives, change.

These means of grace or works of piety, especially as nested in the church's liturgy, can form us in repentance, faith, and love by focusing our hearts on both the holiness of God and our need for that holiness in our lives. This addresses the "transitive" nature of the affections of the heart by providing the right objects for our attention. To some extent, the liturgy not only forms these affections, but expresses them as well. Wesley reminds us, though, that liturgical expression of our heart is not enough. We also need a way to express these affections of our heart beyond the doors of the church. That is the purpose of the "works of mercy": They provide outlets for the expression of our religious affections.

The Works of Mercy: Completing the Cycle of Holiness by Expressing Our Hearts

Repentance, faith, and love are orientations of our hearts. But if we are to take these religious affections seriously, they need to find expression in our actions. We understand this same idea when we say such things as "If you really loved me, you would . . ." Each of us could fill in some duty we would expect of someone claiming to love us. So what kind of actions should define a Christian? What kinds of works could be termed works of love or, as Wesley called them, *works of mercy*?

No one can give a more profound answer to these questions

than Jesus did when he said, "Do to others as you would have them do to you" (Matt. 7:12), which is rightly called the "golden rule." In some places in scripture, such as Matthew 25:31-40, we can find attempts to further specify the kinds of actions that this "golden rule" would entail; Wesley often echoed the commands (for instance) to feed the hungry, clothe the naked, visit the imprisoned and the sick, entertain the stranger, and make disciples among all nations (Matthew 28:19).[11]

How might we embody the charges in Wesley's General Rules today? Our answers will be as diverse as the various circumstances in which we find ourselves. For some, "Do no harm" might mean no longer driving after drinking, or perhaps entering a program to curb the anger that leads to abuse of one's spouse or children. "Do good" might mean working at a Habitat for Humanity house, or it may mean teaching a Sunday school class, helping to care for a disabled person, or being an overseas missionary. We see here that there are many ways of living a life of gratitude and, in so doing, praising God. What enables the process is not only God's grace but our willingness. When we follow Wesley's three simple rules, we are expressing the life that God has formed within us, and we are freed to use our discernment and our knowledge of the world around us to determine just how we will live out this call.

All of this discussion about "rules" and "works," however, might lead us to overlook the fundamental nature of Wesley's vision of Christianity: the primacy of the life of the heart. In his 1745 letter to "John Smith," Wesley warned that "faith working by love" should not degenerate into a works righteousness:

> I would rather say faith is productive of all Christian *holiness* than of all Christian *practice*; because men are so exceeding apt to rest in practice, so called, I mean in outside religion; whereas true religion is eminently seated in the heart, renewed in the image of him that created us.[12]

Wesley knew that it is always a temptation to define Christianity by outwardly observable behaviors, such as church attendance or going to Bible studies. As he constantly guarded against such shallow understandings, so must we.

In his sermon "On Zeal," Wesley exhorts his readers to be more zealous for holy tempers or affections than for works of mercy or even works of piety, for it is the holy tempers that make the works possible.[13] In a sermon written in the last year of his life, "On the Wedding Garment," Wesley describes holiness by reminding us that "the only thing that counts is faith working through love" (Gal. 5:6). Such a text might occasion a moralistic emphasis on action, but Wesley takes this as an occasion to emphasize the centrality of the heart in Christianity. The first work in which this faith is to engage is to produce "love to God and all mankind; and by this love every holy and heavenly temper. In particular, lowliness, meekness, gentleness, temperance, and long-suffering."[14] Here even Christian "works" are described in the most basic terms as that which produces "lowliness," or spiritual poverty, or repentance.

In this emphasis on the heart, Wesley is but once again reinforcing the message of scripture. After all, it was not Wesley but St. Paul who said: "If I give away all my possessions, and if I hand over my body so that I may boast, but do not have love, I gain nothing" (1 Cor. 13:3).

The "House of Religion" Image: Logical, Not Temporal, Connections

The fact that Wesley used a three-part image to summarize the central truths of Christianity—and used this image to show how these truths are linked theologically—does not mean that we will always experience repentance, faith, and love in such a neat and distinguishable sequence. The distinction we need to recognize is the difference between logical connections and temporal connections. Let me give an example to illustrate.

It is quite possible, for instance, that a child would grow up in a congregation in which Christian love is abundant because the adults in that congregation have understood and embodied the gospel. The child may show signs of being a loving child because she has been around so many positive role models. The child learns that loving is the best way to live, and so he or she starts living that way. Only later in the child's life might the child understand that this agape love can be sustained only by understanding its sources: the death of Christ on the cross and his glorious resurrection. The felt need for repentance might not come until she is well along in the Christian life.

But there will come a time (if the congregation's worship and life together is as it should be) that the child will no longer be able to skate through life on the borrowed love of the community. Sooner or later the child will grow up and confront her own sinfulness and be driven to the wellsprings of God's forgiving grace directly. Then she will know that it was the cross of Christ that made possible the love she had experienced earlier in her life. This is part of the maturing and growing process.

In this example, the first thing encountered in time was the love of the community, and the logic of how that love developed was understood only later. This does not mean that the love experienced was not generated in the way Wesley specified, namely, by the cross of Christ. Wesley's vision of the *logical* order of the Christian life, as expressed in the house image, is not violated or negated by someone's experiencing these stages in a different *temporal* order.

We can appreciate the convenience of travel by automobile without understanding everything about internal combustion engines. But if we do not have a minimal knowledge about what makes them work, such as that they need gas periodically, we will not go far. The same is true of the Christian life. We do not have to know much to experience love from others, but if we are going to sustain that love in our own lives, we need to know more. To use another example, we might say that trying to live a life of Christian love without consciously trying to grow it (through attendance to the means of grace) and effectively expressing it (through the works of mercy) is like spending all of your capital instead of investing it and generating more: sooner or later you end up bankrupt.

The same caution about imposing a rigid order on the way our spiritual lives develop (even while having faith in the underlying logic of the process) can be seen in other real-life experiences of believers. Tom Albin has studied the diaries of many early Methodists and found that a great many claimed to have been converted not at a massive outdoor evangelism event, but at the communion rail.[15] In another inversion of what might be expected, many people can testify to times when they set out to do what they thought were going to be "works of mercy"—acts that expressed their love to some unfortunate person—and turned out to do less "expressing" of love than experiencing that formed love within them. (Hence their experience was more of a "work of piety.") The "work" trip that the youth group takes can sometimes build more fellowship than so-called "fellowship" trips can. God's grace meets us in surprising ways if we are but open to it.

The House of Religion in a World of Religions

Many might look at the world today and, in noting the immigration patterns of the last fifty years, say that the pluralistic and diverse nature of the religious scene today makes Wesley's single-minded emphasis on Christianity a little outmoded. After all, when Muslim and Jew live down the street from the Christian, should not our perspective be open, inclusive, and tolerant? What are we to do with this Wesleyan, Christ-centered way of living in the face of people who believe quite differently from us? Many even question the validity of evangelistic activity. How dare we try to impose our way of life on other people who seem to be getting along fine without living in this house of religion?

Wesley himself lived and worked in a world of diversity that in many ways was similar to ours. To be sure, England in Wesley's time did not have the diversity of other formal world religions as it does today, but it did have what he often called a widespread "heathen" spirit that today we would call "secularism." Wesley did not see people practicing high-minded, well-thought-out patterns of love on an ongoing basis. He saw a world filled with self-centered, prideful, greedy, angry people who were filled with violent lusts, people who eschewed patience and scoffed at gentleness as weakness. Is our world so different?

It might surprise some to learn that John Wesley himself held open the possibility that people of other beliefs might lead the life of love that he was inviting people to lead by drawing them into the house of religion. As opposed to many Christians who have overemphasized the "faith" element of the house—people who have seen it as the house itself instead of the door only—Wesley reminded one of his correspondents that

> I regard even faith itself not as an *end*, but as a *means* only. The end of the commandment is love—of every command, of the whole Christian dispensation. Let this love be attained, by whatever means, and I am content; I desire no more. All is well if we love the Lord our God with all our heart, and our neighbor as ourselves.[16]

When people express a hesitancy to evangelize, then, the question to them should be: "Do you see such a surplus of profound agape love in the world that you see no need to share the good news?" It would be hard for anyone who watches the evening news to say yes to such a question. I think, if we were to be perfectly honest, our hesitancy to witness and evangelize comes more from our own sloth or our prideful fear of being rejected than it does from any sense that the world is loving enough as it is. All too often we hide this indolence and pride behind noble-sounding discussions of "tolerance" and "diversity." I think Jesus is wondering how long we can avert our eyes from the suffering, evil, and hate that so dominate the world before we get off our backsides and make a difference.

Yes, for Wesley it was theoretically possible that people might achieve agape love by some other means, by some other faith scheme or philosophy. But Wesley saw Christianity as the best hope for living such a life that he had yet encountered. He saw the porch of repentance and the door of faith in the forgiveness of sins as the way that was actually, and not just theoretically, bringing about changed lives, lives burning with love.

In the end, of course, it is God who will judge who has lived the kind of lives that we were created for, lives marked by sacrificial service to others. Those judgments are in God's hands, and we can be sure that we will be held accountable for walking by the light that we have been given. Wesley warns his hearers that they should "expect to achieve no ends without using the means."[17] Do not hope or expect that a life of love will be yours by floating along in the mainstream of the culture. We need to follow the path that has been revealed to us: worship the God that has been revealed to us, use the means of grace, and practice the works of mercy. If we engaged in a lifelong friendly "competition" with other Christians—and people of other world religions—as to who could be the most loving, I do not think that there could be anything that would please Wesley, and God, more.

Summary: The House of Religion and the Life of the Heart

From all that we have said, we can see that Wesley's "heart religion" is intrinsically social and grounded in the truths of the Christian tradition. It is in the local congregation that repentance is made more permanent, that faith is deepened, and that love is generated and directed to expression. If the central purpose of the local church is fulfilled—if people truly worship God through a well-balanced liturgy and program—then the Christians who worship there will have the virtues or character traits that they are called to have. These Christians will embody the "house of religion" by showing forth the humility that comes from repentance; the gratitude, trust, and peace that come from having faith that our sins are forgiven; and the whole "fruit of the spirit"—love, joy, peace, patience, kindness, generosity, faithfulness, gentleness, and self-control—that grows in the soil of humble, Christian trust.

Reconsidering the hopes and fears that we started with in chapter 1, we can now see that following a heart religion does not necessarily lead to a self-delusional life of individualistic navel-gazing and spiritual pulse-taking. Repentance is not just feeling bad about ourselves; it is being energized to change because we have a new vision of reality. Faith is not some vague assent to the universe; it is a trust that our sins are forgiven. Love is not some unattainable mystic state of elevation; it is the actions in the world that we take, especially towards our enemies, out of gratitude for the love that has been shown us.

The realized righteousness of the religious affections is shown when love, reverence, humility, and "every other holy and heavenly temper"[18] are displayed as integral parts of the character of the believer. This is seen succinctly in Wesley's "Sermon on the Mount, IX" where he says:

"Seek the kingdom of God and his righteousness." Righteousness is the fruit of God's reigning in the heart. And what is righteousness but love? The love of God and of all mankind, flowing from faith in Jesus Christ, and producing humbleness of mind, meekness, gentleness, long-suffering, patience, deadness to the world; and every right disposition of heart toward God and toward man. And by these it produces all holy actions, whatsoever are lovely or of good report; whatsoever works of faith and labour of love are acceptable to God and profitable to man.

"His righteousness." This is all his righteousness still: it is his own free gift to us, for the sake of Jesus Christ the righteous, through whom alone it is purchased for us. And it is his work: it is he alone that worketh it in us by the inspiration of his Holy Spirit.[19]

Knowing that we are living such a life of love and joy and peace allows us to speak about the "assurance" of faith. Assurance is not some occult feeling or sensation; it is seeing the fruit of the Spirit active in our lives and thereby knowing that we are God's children. If we take our own feelings as the objects of our affections, we obviously will be caught up in a self-defeating, vicious circle. Wesley's vision, which emphasizes taking only certain objects for our affections, and which specifies the behaviors toward which these affections should dispose us, does not allow for an individualistic religion of pure feeling.

When, through the prompting and guiding of the Holy Spirit, the sinner focuses on the awesome, forgiving love of God, which makes him aware of his own sinfulness, the affection of repentance or sorrow for sins grows. This leads to trusting in the God who forgives sin. In turn, this faith leads us into the life of holiness in which our love and joy focus on God, and we are disposed to act in the best interests of our neighbors. John Wesley's heart religion is a necessarily relational, spirit-dependent, and communal vision of the righteousness of Christ enfleshed on earth.

Pertinent Sermons of John Wesley

To understand the variety of struggles that continue to be a part of the Christian life even as we are "going on to perfection," see "Wandering Thoughts (sermon 41); "Satan's Devices" (sermon 42); "The Wilderness State" (sermon 46); and "Heaviness through Manifold Temptations" (sermon 47). To see how even Christians need to continue in the act of repentance throughout their lives, see "On Sin in Believers" (sermon 13) and "The Repentance of Believers" (sermon 14). For discussions of the works of piety and works of mercy see "The Means of Grace" (sermon 16) and "The Scripture Way of Salvation" (sermon 43). On assurance, see "The Witness of the Spirit I and II" (sermons 10 and 11) and "The Witness of Our Own Spirit" (sermon 12).

Wesleyan Hymn on the "Means of Grace"

"Come, Sinners, to the Gospel Feast" (# 616 UMH)

> Come, sinners, to the gospel feast,
> let every soul be Jesus' guest.
> Ye need not one be left behind,
> for God hath bid all humankind.

> Do not begin to make excuse;
> ah! do not you his grace refuse;
> your worldly cares and pleasures leave,
> and take what Jesus hath to give.

> Come and partake the gospel feast,
> be saved from sin, in Jesus rest;
> O taste the goodness of our God,
> and eat his flesh and drink his blood.

See him set forth before your eyes;
behold the bleeding sacrifice;
his offered love make haste to embrace,
and freely now be saved by grace.

Ye who believe his record true
shall sup with him and he with you;
come to the feast, be saved from sin,
for Jesus waits to take you in.

Notes on "Come, Sinners, to the Gospel Feast"

This hymn was written in 1747 and is based on Jesus' parable of the "great dinner" (Luke 14:16-24) where the people who were invited to a feast all made excuses and never showed up. In the parable, the invitation then was extended to all. The story provides a beautiful image to express how, for Charles Wesley, the communion table is open to all who seek a new life with Christ.

Verse One: All of the sinners in the world—in other words, all of humanity—are invited to this gospel feast. The feast is, of course, the bread and the wine of communion.

Verse Two: Do not refuse his grace, Charles says, implying that we are capable of doing so. This reflects the basic Wesleyan emphasis on human freedom—we are made capable of saying "no" to God, though God is always asking all to the table of fellowship.

Verse Three: When we "rest" in Jesus—trust that his death has forgiven our sins—we are saved from sin. That is what makes it possible for us to "taste" the goodness of our God.

Verse Four: The sacrifice of Jesus on the cross is brought before us when we take communion. The grace that flowed to us freely from that act calls us into that life of love in imitation of him.

Verse Five: "Ye who believe his record true"—all who trust in the gospel story—shall enjoy the fellowship of God's feast.

Jesus is always waiting; we need but turn to him.

Another Wesleyan sacramental hymn is "O the Depth of Love Divine" (# 627 UMH). These two hymns obviously relate to the "works of piety," but there are also several relating to the "works of mercy." See, for example, "Forth in Thy Name, O Lord" (# 438 UMH) or "A Charge to Keep I Have" (# 413 UMH).

Perhaps no other piece of Wesleyan literature can summarize the virtues of the "house of religion" better than the so-called "covenant prayer." It is not entirely original to John Wesley (and this once again shows his continuity with tradition), but he adapted it as an expression of what the Christian life is supposed to be all about. As a prayer, it expresses our basic posture in life: looking to God not only with humility and reverence, but also with the eager desire to respond to God's grace, which flows from our gratitude over being loved and forgiven. In the words themselves, we see the bold commitment that Christ has called forth by purchasing us on the cross, a commitment to use our freedom to lead a life of humble love. Finally, because this prayer is scriptural, it is emblematic of Wesley's theology; its basic thrust expresses a scripture passage that can be found often in the writings of John Wesley: "whether you eat or drink or whatever you do, do everything for the glory of God" (1 Cor. 10:31). I reproduce below the version of this prayer that is found in the *United Methodist Hymnal* (# 607).

> I am no longer my own, but thine.
> Put me to what thou wilt, rank me with whom thou
>   wilt.
> Put me to doing, put me to suffering.
> Let me be employed by thee or laid aside for thee,
> exalted for thee or brought low by thee.
> Let me be full, let me be empty.
> Let me have all things, let me have nothing.
> I freely and heartily yield all things

to thy pleasure and disposal.
And now, O glorious and blessed God,
Father, Son, and Holy Spirit,
thou art mine, and I am thine. So be it.
And the covenant which I have made on earth,
let it be ratified in heaven. Amen.

Suggestions for Further Reading

Steve Harper's *Devotional Life in the Wesleyan Tradition: A Workbook* (Nashville: Upper Room, 1995) gives a very helpful look at Wesley's "means of grace." David Lowes Watson has written several books on "Christian conference" and accountability groups. See his *The Early Methodist Class Meeting* (Nashville: Discipleship Resources, 1985) and his *Covenant Discipleship* (Nashville: Discipleship Resources, 1989). Richard J. Foster's books *Celebration of Discipline* (San Francisco: Harper and Row, 1978) and *Prayer: Finding the Heart's True Home* (San Francisco: Harper, 1992) are very helpful. One of the best books on prayer is *Beginning to Pray* by Anthony Bloom (New York: Paulist, 1970). For searching the scripture for spiritual formation see *Shaped by the Word* by Robert Mulholland (Nashville: Upper Room, 1985).

Questions for Reflection or Discussion

• What comes to mind when you say (or hear someone else say), "I am going to church?" What difference would it make to say, "I am going to worship God?"

• What would it be like to see your weekly worship as a time to refocus your heart on God? What would you do differently? How would your attitudes be different from your present attitude?

• When we think of doing "Christian" things in the world, we sometimes think only of the most dramatic examples, like Mother Teresa's work with the dying in India. What are some of the "works of mercy" that you could do right in your own church, your own neighborhood, your own house, your own family?

• When you consider real-life people to whom you have shown love, are they more likely to be your family and friends, or do you also reach out to "enemies"? What specific "enemy" can you show love to today? Would it make a difference in your motivation if you can remember that in showing agape love, you are showing God's holiness to the world?

• If your "enemy" rejects your offer of love how can you persevere in love and avoid being cynical or giving up? Consider a real-life example and how you might deal with rejection or scorn. Think about the distinction between being successful and being faithful. What does that distinction have to do with our attempts to love our enemy?

Notes

[1] See Wesley's *Works*, vol. IX, 67–75.

[2] For a fuller explanation and discussion of the "means of grace," see Steve Harper's very helpful book *Devotional Life in the Wesleyan Tradition: A Workbook* (Nashville: Upper Room, 1995).

[3] See the *United Methodist Hymnal*, pages 50–54, for an excellent example.

[4] See Wesley's sermon 16 on the means of grace and Harper's book for more on the instituted means of grace.

[5] See *John Wesley's Sunday Service of the Methodists in North America* with an Introduction by James F. White. (Nashville: The United Methodist Publishing House and the United Methodist Board of Higher Education and Ministry, 1984). This is a commemorative reprint published by *Quarterly Review*.

[6] See especially the books by Anthony Bloom and Richard J. Foster in the "Suggestions for Further Reading" section above.

[7] One excellent program is the Disciple Bible Study Program,

published by The United Methodist Publishing House. This program takes the Wesleyan view of Bible study, namely, that the point of studying it is not to compile a lot of facts about the Bible but to grow disciples of Jesus. Creating disciples is, of course, the final point of the whole process of growing in holiness.

8 There are, of course, a wide variety of theories about the manner of Christ's presence in the bread and wine. See Alister McGrath's *Christian Theology: An Introduction* (Cambridge: Blackwell, 1994), chapter 14, for a representative sampling, but this should be pursued only if you remember that theories about communion are not as important as participation in the mystery.

9 See chapter 4 on fasting in Foster's *Celebration of Discipline* (San Francisco: Harper, 1978).

10 See the works by David Lowes Watson mentioned in "Suggestions for Further Reading."

11 Compare Matthew 25:31-40 and Matthew 28:19 with Wesley's "General Rules," *Works*, vol. 9, 69–73, and "The Scripture Way of Salvation," sermon 43, 166.

12 Letter of December 30, 1745, *Works*, vol. XXVI, 179.

13 Sermon 92, 313.

14 Sermon 127, "On the Wedding Garment," 147.

15 See his dissertation at Cambridge University, still in progress at the time of this writing.

16 Letters, June 25, 1746, 203.

17 In "The Nature of Enthusiasm," Wesley's *Works*, vol. II, 56, Wesley terms any who would try to attain the end of holiness without using the means of grace an "enthusiast," i.e., someone who has gone "overboard" with inner experience or supposed "revelations."

18 Sermon 20, "The Lord Our Righteousness," 452–453.

19 Sermon 29, 642–643.

Glossary of Terms

Faith: Has two relevant meanings: (1) the doctrinal truths that a believer agrees with, such as when we say "The Apostles' Creed contains the essentials of the Christian faith"; and, (2) the sense of personal trust that marks the everyday life of a believer. Both meanings are included in what Wesley meant by the "door of faith."

General Rules: The three basic guidelines that John Wesley gave to those who wanted to be good disciples of Christ: (1) do no harm and avoid evil; (2) do good of every possible sort to all people; and (3) do the works of piety.

Heart: Not just our "feelings" but that deepest part of human reality that defines who we are in our essence. It basically is understood in terms of the "affections" or emotions it contains, and its nature is elicited by answering such questions as "What do you fear?" "What do you love?" "What do you take joy in?" "What brings you peace?"

Holiness: When used to describe the presence of God, holiness refers to an overwhelming awe- and fear-inducing experience of the purity and majesty of God. A glimpse of this is what most powerfully brings about repentance. As a goal for human life, holiness is best understood as a life defined by agape, or self-giving love.

Orthodoxy: The correct or right beliefs or doctrines that define a religion, such as belief in the divinity of Christ or the idea that Christ died for our sins. Orthodoxy is that part of "faith" that can be put down on paper.

Orthokardia: The right heart. Having a right heart means having all of the "religious affections" (such as the "fruit of the Spirit" of Galatians 5:22-23). This entails having the right beliefs (orthodoxy) so that the affections are taking the right objects. (For instance, our joy has the right objects if it comes in serving the God revealed in Christ, not in having material possessions, or our thankfulness has the right object if it grows from God's forgiveness of our sins and not from our favorite football team's current winning streak.) It also entails doing the right actions (orthopraxis) since the affections are not truly religious if they do not dispose us to behave in certain ways (your thankfulness leads you to serve in a local church, your love compels you to work with the handicapped, and so forth).

Orthopraxis: The right actions or works. This is not understood as something that comes as a precondition for salvation—we cannot earn the forgiveness of sins that comes from the cross of Christ. The right actions flow out of the Christian affections of the renewed heart. They basically are the actions we do as we try to love God and love our neighbor.

Repentance: Turning from a life defined by rebellion, pride, and sin to a life marked by obedience, humility, and love.

Standard Sermons: The sermons collected by John Wesley to be used as guidelines for people trying to lead a Christian life.

Works of Mercy: Sometimes called *works of love*, these are how we express our gratitude and love to God and our forgiveness and love to our neighbors. These include actions such as feeding the hungry, clothing the naked, giving shelter to the homeless, and visiting the sick and those in prison.

Works of Piety: The means of grace. Those things which help us develop the right heart, those actions which God uses as instruments for shaping believers lives with grace. These include baptism, communion, public worship, prayer, fasting, searching the scriptures, and Christian conference (meeting with other believers to hold each other accountable).

Gregory S. Clapper is associate professor in the Chapman-Benson Chair of Christian Faith and Philosophy at Huntingdon College, Montgomery, Alabama. Prior to this position he was the senior pastor of Trinity United Methodist Church, Waverly, Iowa. Previously, he served as associate professor of Religion and Philosophy at Westmar College in Le Mars, Iowa.

The author, a native of Park Ridge, Illinois, holds degrees from Carthage College (B.A.), the University of Wisconsin-Milwaukee (M.A.), Garrett-Evangelical Theological Seminary (M.Div.), and Emory University (Ph.D.).

Dr. Clapper is married to Jody, and they have two children: Laura and Jenna.